Summit Guide

to the

Cascade Volcanoes

Summit Guide
to the
Cascade Volcanoes

Jeff Smoot

Chockstone Press
Evergreen, Colorado

SUMMIT GUIDE TO THE CASCADE VOLCANOES

© 1992 Jeff Smoot. All rights reserved. Printed in the United States of America. No part of this book may be used or reproduced in any manner whatsoever without written permission of the publisher, except in the case of brief quotations embodied in critical articles and reviews.

Cover photo of Mount Hood by Alan Kearney

PUBLISHED AND DISTRIBUTED BY:
Chockstone Pres, Inc.
P.O. Box 3505
Evergreen, Colo. 80439

ISBN: 0-934641-25-0

WARNING: CLIMBING IS A SPORT WHERE YOU MAY BE SERIOUSLY INJURED OR DIE.
READ THIS BEFORE YOU USE THIS BOOK.

This guidebook is a compilation of unverified information gathered from many different sources. The author cannot assure the accuracy of any of the information in this book, including topos and route descriptions, difficulty ratings and protection ratings. These may be incorrect or misleading and it is impossible for any one author to climb all the routes to confirm the information about each route. Also, ratings of climbing difficulty and danger are always subjective and depend on the physical characteristics, experience, technical ability, confidence and physical fitness of the climber who supplied the rating. Therefore, be warned that you must exercise your own judgment on where a climbing route goes, its difficulty and your ability to safely protect yourself from the risks of climbing. Examples of some of these risks are: falling due to technical difficulty or due to natural hazards such as holds breaking, falling rock and ice avalanches, climbing equipment dropped by other climbers, hazards of weather and lightning, your own equipment failure, and failure of fixed protection.

You should not depend on any information contained in this book for your personal safety; your safety depends on your own good judgment, based on experience and a realistic assessment of your climbing ability as well as weather and route conditions. If you have any doubt as to your ability to safely climb a route described in this book, do not attempt it.

The following are some ways to make your use of this book safer:

1. **CONSULTATION:** You should consult with climbers and other sources (U.S. Forest Service; National Park Service) about the difficulty and danger of a particular climb prior to attempting it. Most local climbers are glad to give advice on routes in their area and we suggest that you contact locals to confirm ratings and safety of particular routes and to obtain first-hand information about a route chosen from this book.

2. **INSTRUCTION:** Most climbing areas have local climbing instructors and guides available. We recommend that you engage an instructor or guide to learn safety techniques and to become familiar with the routes and hazards of the areas described in this book. Even after you are proficient in climbing safely, occasional use of a guide is a safe way to raise your climbing standard and learn advanced techniques. Some guide services are listed in the appendix of this book.

Be aware of the following specific potential hazards which could arise in using this book:

1. **MISDESCRIPTIONS OF ROUTES:** If you climb a route and you have a doubt as to where the route may go, you should not go on unless you are sure that you can go that way safely. Route descriptions and topos in this book may be inaccurate or misleading. Route descriptions change throughout the seasons due to weather and snow conditions.

2. **INCORRECT DIFFICULTY RATING:** A route may, in fact, be more difficult than the rating indicates. Do not be lulled into a false sense of security by the difficulty rating.

THERE ARE NO WARRANTIES, WHETHER EXPRESS OR IMPLIED, THAT THIS GUIDEBOOK IS ACCURATE OR THAT THE INFORMATION CONTAINED IN IT IS RELIABLE. THERE ARE NO WARRANTIES OF FITNESS FOR A PARTICULAR PURPOSE OR THAT THIS GUIDE IS MERCHANTABLE. YOUR USE OF THIS BOOK INDICATES YOUR ASSUMPTION OF THE RISK THAT IT MAY CONTAIN ERRORS AND IS AN ACKNOWLEDGEMENT OF YOUR OWN SOLE RESPONSIBILITY FOR YOUR CLIMBING SAFETY.

Preface

This guide originally was intended to cover all routes up each of the Cascade volcanoes. However, as the project progressed, it became evident that such a guide would be encyclopedic in volume and contain much too much information for those most likely to use it. Realizing that the majority of climbers don't seek too much detail about remote, unpopular, unaesthetic or dangerous routes, the focus of this guide was modified. Included are detailed descriptions, maps and photos with overlays for the easiest, most popular, most accessible and most aesthetic routes up each of the Cascade volcanoes included. This guide discusses the less popular, less aesthetic, more remote and more dangerous routes, but in summary fashion, with references to other guidebooks and journals for those seeking something "off the beaten track."

Hopefully, this guide will provide sufficient information to get you where you want to go, provided you want to go to the summit of any of the major Cascade Range volcanic peaks.

Acknowledgements

If anything is true in guidebook writing: "It's not what you know but who you know." This guide is not solely the result of an individual effort by the author, but rather a compilation of efforts of many individuals. Without the assistance of others, whether in providing route information, photographs, reviewing the manuscript or simply providing the name of someone with useful information or photographs, preparing this guide would have been an impossible task. I am greatly indebted to Eldon Altizer, Matt Arksey, Virginia Baker, Tom Bauman, Tom Bell, Alex Bertulis, Jim Blilie, Tim Boyer, James Bull, Jack Cameron, Riley Caton, Mark Dale, Bill Dengler, Nick Dodge, Steve Doty, Nancy Eberle, Phil Ershler, Bruce Fairley, Ed Hall, Brent Harris, Ken Henshaw, Dave Hirst, Wally Kerchum, George Larsen, Jeff Leisy, Darryl Lloyd, Royal Mannion, Christopher Mason, Dee Molenaar, Janice Naragon, Larry Nielson, Jon Olson, Garry Olson, Barbara Samora, Don Serl, Thomas Servatius, Steve Sorseth, Ray Smutek, Bill Soule, Oliver Thomae, Richard Vance, Frank Vicen, Leif Voeltz, Mike Volk, Ron Warfield, Doug Weaver, Howard Weaver, Jim Wickwire, Margaret Yates and Michael Zanger. Special thanks to Matt Keyser, who envisioned this guide but had the foresight to abandon it to me, and to Pat Gentry, for her invaluable proofreading and fact-finding efforts. Great assistance was provided by personnel of the U.S. Geological Survey Ice and Climate Study Project, Mt. Baker-Snoqualmie National Forest, Gifford Pinchot National Forest, Mt. Hood National Forest, Shasta-Trinity National Forest, Washington Department of Recreation, Mount Rainier National Park, Lassen Volcanic National Park, British Columbia Forest Service and British Columbia Mountaineering Council. Thanks also to The Mountaineers and to the Northwest Interpretive Association for use of their excellent outdoor libraries. If I have forgotten someone, my sincere apology.

Thanks as always to my family and publisher for their enduring patience during the four years spent writing this guide.

Table of Contents

Introduction 1

The Cascade Volcanoes 9

Volcano Climbing 15

Part 1: British Columbia

Chapter One: Mount Garibaldi 29

Part 2: Washington

Chapter Two: Mount Baker 39
Chapter Three: Glacier Peak 51
Chapter Four: Mount Rainier 63
Chapter Five: Little Tahoma Peak 81
Chapter Six: Mount St. Helens 85
Chapter Seven: Mount Adams 91

Part 3: Oregon

Chapter Eight: Mount Hood	*103*
Chapter Nine: Mount Jefferson	*117*
Chapter Ten: Three Fingered Jack	*127*
Chapter Eleven: Mount Washington	*131*
Chapter Twelve: Three Sisters	*135*
Chapter Thirteen: Broken Top	*149*
Chapter Fourteen: Mount Bachelor	*155*
Chapter Fifteen: Mount Thielsen	*157*
Chapter Sixteen: Mount McLoughlin	*159*

Part 4: California

Chapter Seventeen: Mount Shasta	*161*
Chapter Eighteen: Mount Lassen	*175*

Appendix *178*

Bibliography *179*

Climbers enjoy a sunrise from the Ingraham Glacier on Mount Rainier.

Photo: Mark Dale

Introduction

The volcanoes of the Cascade Range are magnets to the adventuresome populations who live nearby. Puget Sound lowlanders are treated to a panorama of mountains, but are drawn to the giants – Mounts Baker and Rainier. Columbia River Gorge and northwestern Oregon residents likewise hold Mount Hood in high esteem. Residents of central Oregon are treated to a splendid panorama of high volcanoes. Northern Californians cannot escape the dominating presence of Mount Shasta. These are the "power points," if you will, of the Pacific Northwest. Without going into the physical, mystical, psychological and philosophical attractions of the big peaks, suffice it to say that millions visit the volcano parks and wilderness areas each year, and, like a rite of passage, thousands climb at least one of the Cascade volcanoes during their lifetimes. For others, the lure of the high volcanoes does not end with one ascent, but becomes a lifelong obsession. Some return to the same mountain year after year; others climb each peak only once by the easiest route; some climb only the "classic" routes; and others climb whatever and whenever possible.

Due to the limited scope of this guide, many volcanic peaks within the Cascade Range have been excluded, including many "minor" summits, volcanic remnants, and a plethora of cinder cones. As a general rule, this guide covers only glaciated volcanic peaks and those rising above 10,000 feet. Thus, some impressive high peaks are left out. Though there are numerous significant volcanic peaks in the Cascade Range, most have no glaciers, nor do they presently rise above 10,000 feet. A few exceptions to this rule have been made for lower volcanic peaks, such as Mount St. Helens, Mount Washington, Three Fingered Jack, Mount Thielsen and Mount McLoughlin. These peaks were included because of their high visibility, popularity or geological significance – or just for the heck of it, in a couple of cases.

This guide does not provide instruction for would-be mountain climbers. Those who want to learn to climb should consult manuals written for that purpose and take a mountaineering instruction course before attempting to climb any route on a Cascade volcano, particularly those involving glacier travel or technical rock or ice climbing. (Mountaineering instruction books and climbing guide services are listed in the appendix for the reader's convenience.)

A warning to the unwary: While thousands of mountain ascents are safely accomplished each year, mountain climbing, and particularly glacier and volcano climbing, involve inherent dangers which, although not always obvious, are always present. Many mountain accidents occur when inexperienced climbers attempt routes that are too difficult for them, or exercise poor judgment in the face of changing circumstances, and particularly because of fatigue-induced error. However, many climbing accidents occur by chance, due to unforeseen avalanches, rockfall, rapid weather changes, human frailty and other objective hazards. Climbing accidents are usually avoidable with the use of good judgment developed through experience, but not always. There is no substitute for experience – not even a well-written guide. Most of the routes contained in this guide are no place for inexperienced climbers.

If this guide at times seems preoccupied with the hazards associated with mountaineering, it is because the author fears that non-climbers with inadequate experience or equipment might buy this book and head straight for the mountains. This is not an unfounded fear, considering ill-equipped tourists sometimes head off from Paradise for the summit of Mount Rainier ("It seems so close!"), and even though most turn back before they reach Camp Muir, the possibility for tragedy still exists. "Tourist" climbers have died on Mount Rainier, Mount Hood, Mount Shasta and elsewhere. A woman is reported to have reached the summit of Mount Hood wearing high heels. While this is an admirable accomplishment, it is also quite scary.

Inexperienced climbers who read this book and are inspired to climb these peaks, please, get professional help! Hire a guide service or take a climbing instruction course first.

Using This Guide

This guide does not presume to know every feature of every route on every volcano in the Cascade Range. Mountains – especially the volcanoes – change from season to season. Evidence of this is the very recent rockfall on the Winthrop Glacier on Mount Rainier. In September 1989, an estimated 2.6 million cubic yards of rock broke loose from the Curtis Ridge-Russell Cliff portion of the mountain. A larger rockfall, estimated at about 14 million cubic yards, fell from the north face of Little Tahoma Peak onto the Emmons Glacier in 1963. And, of course, Mount St. Helens today bears little resemblance to the once-graceful cone that graced the Cascade Range was prior to 1980. These are examples of large-scale changes that have occured during recorded history; however, minor rockfalls, ice avalanches, or even weather or seasonal changes will alter the nature and course of a mountain route. These are not, after all, rock climbs on Yosemite granite. A route that follows ice gullies one weekend may involve difficult technical climbing on frighteningly loose rock the next. A route that climbed snow-covered glaciers one month may be hideously crevassed or impassable the next. Changes can and do occur overnight. Snow slopes that are stable in the early morning can avalanche copiously in the afternoon. Inability to adjust to changing conditions can be hazardous, even deadly, for the unwary.

As with any other climbing guide, the routes detailed here are approximate only, and are based upon historical and popular usage, not correctness or exactness of line. There are no dotted lines to follow on the mountains; you have to pick the best and safest routes yourself. All route descriptions and directions assume you are facing the mountain and/or your direction of travel. All distances, angles of slopes, ratings and directions are approximate unless otherwise stated.

Each section of the guide contains maps showing road and trail access to the volcanoes. You should not rely on these maps, photos and drawings except to help guide you to your mountain from the lowlands and show you the approximate line of ascent. The maps and drawings are not exact, and cannot substitute for U.S. Geological Survey topographic maps, skilled compass use and careful routefinding learned through experience. Camp and bivouac sites mentioned in the text and shown on maps and photographs are merely suggested or previously used sites, and, with the exception of designated wilderness campsites, may not be safe or even comfortable.

Introduction 3

Generally, you'll find the standard route to the top of the peak described first and in detail. This doesn't mean it's the easiest, or best, simply that it's most-often used. Other sought-after routes also are described in some detail. Less worthy routes are described briefly; if you wish to learn more about these routes, consult the references listed in the bibliography. In general, routes are presented counter-clockwise around the mountain beginning with the standard route.

These route descriptions should not be deemed absolutely precise or correct. Numerous variations likely have been and will be climbed, whether for the sake of climbing something different or to avoid hazards or obstacles, and all variations cannot possibly be listed here. On some routes, each successive party climbs a slightly different variation of "the route," taking detours all along the way. For most of the routes in this guide, there is no "correct route;" it goes wherever you have to go to climb the peak. Generally, if a route climbs a specific feature of the mountain, it will be described in detail; when several possible variations exist, less detail will be provided. Things change, and climbers must use their own judgment when deciding which route to climb.

On approaches, be aware that the density of the surrounding forests diminishes as one moves farther south. If you don't follow a precise course (i.e, the trail) on approaches to Mount Baker and Glacier Peak, and other northern peaks, you will become hopelessly lost or entangled. Stay on trails and climbers' paths, or suffer the consequences.

A large part of the climbing experience, as any wilderness travel, is discovery and exploration. To that end, this guide won't reveal everything in minute detail. Hopefully, users will get where they want to go, but won't miss out on the best part of the climbing experience – the adventure – in the process.

Steep ice near the top of Mount Hood's Sandy Glacier Headwall.

Photo: Bill Soule, courtesy Timberline Mountain Guides

Introduction

Ratings

Without trying to invent a new climbing rating system, this guide will rate the general difficulty and seriousness of the volcano routes as follows:

(0) - **No Technical Difficulty.** May not require a rope during optimal conditions. Easy to moderate snow and/or scree, with very minimal glacier travel, if any, and no technical rock. Few unusual objective hazards to worry about. Experienced off-trail hikers and less-experienced climbers usually find these routes fairly simple and straightforward. Bring an ice axe, rope, crampons and maybe a helmet. Examples: Avalanche Gulch (Shasta), West Side (South Sister), Monitor Ridge (St. Helens), South Slope (Adams), Paradise to Camp Muir (Rainier).

(1) - **Easy scrambling or glacier travel,** with few technical challenges or crevasses to be encountered during optimal conditions. Roping up recommended on glacier portion of route. Minimal commitment with minor exposure to hazards. These are good routes for climbers with basic scrambling, snow travel and crevasse rescue experience. Bring a rope, ice axe, crampons, a helmet and maybe a few ice screws. Examples: Cascade Gulch (Shasta), Inter Glacier to Camp Schurman (Rainier), Sitkum Glacier (Glacier Peak), Hogback (Hood).

(2) - **Moderate scrambling or glacier travel,** with abundant crevasses that are not usually difficult to pass, or possibly some rock scrambling (Class 2 or 3). Roping up recommended on glaciers and exposed rock sections. Moderate commitment with increased exposure to hazards. Climbers should have prior glacier and scrambling experience before trying these routes. Bring a rope, ice axe, crampons, helmet, a few ice screws and/or rock pitons, and have crevasse rescue capability. Examples: Warren Glacier (Garibaldi), Emmons Glacier, Disappointment Cleaver (Rainier), Coleman Glacier (Baker), Eliot Glacier (Hood), Whitney Glacier (Shasta).

(3) - **Moderate technical climbing or glacier travel,** with abundant crevasses that may be difficult to pass, and possibly some easy technical rock or ice (Class 3 to 4, possibly some easy Class 5). Greater commitment and exposure to hazards. Belayed climbing may be necessary in places, and roping up on glaciers is highly recommended. Bring a rope, crampons, ice axe, helmet, an assortment of ice screws and/or rock pitons, and have crevasse rescue capability. Examples: Park Glacier (Baker), Tahoma Glacier (Rainier), Hotlam Glacier, Sargents Ridge (Shasta).

(4) - **Difficult technical climbing or glacier travel,** possible moderate technical rock (Class 4 to mid-Class 5) and more difficult ice. Very committing and challenging, with great exposure to hazards. For very experienced climbers only. Bring rope, ice axe and/or specialized ice tools, crampons, helmet, a comprehensive rack of ice and/or rock protection, have crevasse rescue capability, and be prepared for retreat or bivouac. Examples: Siberian Express (Garibaldi), Nisqually Icefall, Mowich Face (Rainier), Coleman Glacier Headwall (Baker), Adams Glacier (Adams), East Arête (North Sister, Middle Sister), Whitney Glacier Icefall (Shasta).

(5) - **Technically extreme climbing,** with difficult and/or committing rock and/or ice climbing and very great exposure to objective hazards. For expert climbers and complete idiots only. Bring rope, ice axe and/or specialized ice tools, crampons, helmet, a comprehensive rack of ice and/or rock protection, have crevasse rescue capability, and be prepared for retreat or bivouac. Examples: Willis Wall, Curtis Ridge (Rainier), Yocum Ridge (Hood), Victory Ridge, Rusk Glacier Headwall (Adams).

This guide also uses the Roman numeral grading system for technical routes. This system takes various factors into account, including difficulty, routefinding, continuity, risk and commitment. Like the technical ratings, these grades assume you are on route during good conditions and know what you are up to. Inexperienced climbers can easily have a Grade V experience on a Grade I route. The Roman numeral system, when used together with the system defined above, will give a very good idea of what a climber may expect on a given technical route. It rates a route's seriousness, and is generally defined as follows:

Grade I - There is little commitment, difficulty or objective danger under ordinary conditions. The entire route may take all day, but the technical climbing will not take very long (perhaps a few hours), and you can turn back fairly easily. Example: North Ridge (Washington); South Ridge (Three Fingered Jack); Northeast Ridge (Thielsen); Hogback (Hood).

Grade II - Technical portions may take a few hours to half a day. There is increased committment, difficulty and exposure to objective hazards. Retreat is not especially difficult. Examples: South Ridge (North Sister), Whitney Glacier Icefall (Shasta).

Grade III - Expect to spend at least half a day on technical portions of route. There is moderate commitment and difficulty; may have higher exposure to objective hazards. Retreat may be time-consuming and difficult. Examples: North Face (Hood), Jefferson Park Glacier (Jefferson), Diller Glacier Headwall (Middle Sister), Casaval Ridge (Shasta).

Grade IV - You could spend all day on the route. It is very committing, technically difficult, and may be very objectively hazardous. Retreat may be very difficult. Be prepared to bivouac. Examples: Coleman Glacier Headwall (Baker), Mowich Face, Liberty Ridge (Rainier).

Grade V - Technical portions of route will take all day, and a bivouac is likely. Expect extreme committment on a technically demanding route. Great exposure to objective dangers. Retreat will be difficult and dangerous. Examples: Willis Wall (Rainier); Yocum Ridge (Hood).

This guide uses the standard decimal rating system (Yosemite Decimal System) for technical rock sections. Climbers unfamiliar with this rating system probably are unfamiliar with the rigors of technical rock climbing, and should stay off of these routes unless accompanied by an experienced leader. In general:

- **Class 1 and 2** represents easy scrambling where the use of hands may or may not be required;
- **Class 3** represents exposed scrambling which, while not especially difficult, may warrant the use of a rope for some;
- **Class 4** represents climbs where belays will likely be used on easy but highly-exposed rock;
- **Class 5.0 through 5.5** represents easy to moderate belayed technical rock climbing where intermediate protection will be placed;

Introduction

- **Class 5.6 through 5.8** represents more difficult technical rock climbing where protection will be placed more frequently;
- **Class 5.9 and above** represent very difficult technical rock climbing that requires a high level of technique and fitness.

Technical rock ratings presently go as high as 5.14 on this scale; fortunately, there are no routes of that difficulty in this guide. In fact, you will be hard-pressed to find a 5.8 route in this guide, and even more fortunate to survive a 5.8 lead on most Cascade volcanoes. Most of the rock climbing contained in this guide is on very poor rock. Some is fairly solid, some is shattered, and some has the consistency of dried mud. Climbing on snow or ice is preferable to rock on most of the Cascade volcanoes, so routes that involve much loose rock are better climbed in winter or early season. Then again, if hideously loose rock is your thing, enjoy!

Technical ice sections will be noted where they exist. A route with steep ice climbing will probably fall under the 3 or 4 category in this guide; frozen waterfalls and ice cliffs usually fall into the 4 or 5 categories. Extreme ice climbing does not exist on any of the Cascade volcanoes under "normal" conditions. However, this does not mean frozen waterfalls and vertical ice cliffs will not be encountered; it means they can usually be avoided for the sake of expediency and safety. You are welcome to attempt frozen waterfalls, ice cliffs and rime ice formations (which sometimes offer a relatively attractive alternative to rotten volcanic rock), but at your peril.

Any route in this guide can be made more difficult, whether by ascending directly over crevasses and ice cliffs rather than skirting them, by climbing over rock buttresses rather than around them, or by climbing during poor weather or winter conditions. All ratings in this guide assume the route is in perfect condition with stable weather and that the climber is taking the easiest and safest possible path, avoiding obvious difficulties and dangers. Winter and poor-weather ascents have additional difficulties and dangers (e.g., ice, increased avalanche danger, frostbite, storms, whiteouts, high winds) that could render the rating used in this guide invalid.

The guide includes a quality rating system, which consists of a star ★ indicating those routes that are deservedly popular. Just because a route doesn't have a star doesn't mean it isn't worth climbing, but routes with stars are, by concensus, usually well worth the trip. This should be useful to visiting climbers and those who climb volcano routes infrequently and want a quality climbing experience.

Warnings of objective hazards are contained throughout this guide. However, the absence of a warning doesn't mean avalanches, rockfall or icefall never occur on a given route, or that nobody has ever been seriously injured or killed on a particular route, only that they are not frequent or regular occurences under ordinary conditions. Nor does "death route" denote an actual fatality on a route (since, for example, no deaths have occured on Willis Wall – yet). Also, "dog route" doesn't mean a dog could actually climb the route, although dogs are frequent (and illegal) visitors to summits of many Cascade volcanoes.

Introduction

This guide also incorporates the following symbols:

 - Highly prone to avalanching.

 - High incidence of rockfall.

 - Exposure to icefall.

The following symbols also appear on maps and photos:

 - "Death route" (i.e., very dangerous and/or frequent accident sites).

 - "Dog route" (i.e., easiest route on the mountain).

This guide provides estimated climbing times for each route. These time estimates are calculated for an average party climbing at a steady pace from high camp to the summit, unless otherwise stated in the route description. Descent times are not be included except in a few instances. These estimated ascent times assume the party is up to the difficulties of the route and that they encounter good climbing conditions. Weather, crevasses, poor snow, ice and rock conditions, slow climbers and other factors may render the time estimates invalid. A strong climbing team may take much less time than the estimate provided for a given route, while another team may take more time. Don't try to "beat the clock," but if you are way behind schedule, don't press on into a forced bivouac or worse. Time estimates in this guide are pretty generous, assuming you will take longer than an average party.

The rating systems used in this guide are to help climbers chose routes that are appropriate for them and to let them know what to expect on a given route. They are not an exact technical rating. Just because a route is rated ⓞ in this guide does not mean it will never be difficult or dangerous. Once again, these difficulty ratings assume perfect conditions, and are provided merely to assist climbers in choosing appropriate routes for their level of ability and experience. They are not intended as an indication of actual difficulty, safety, or as a guarantee of success.

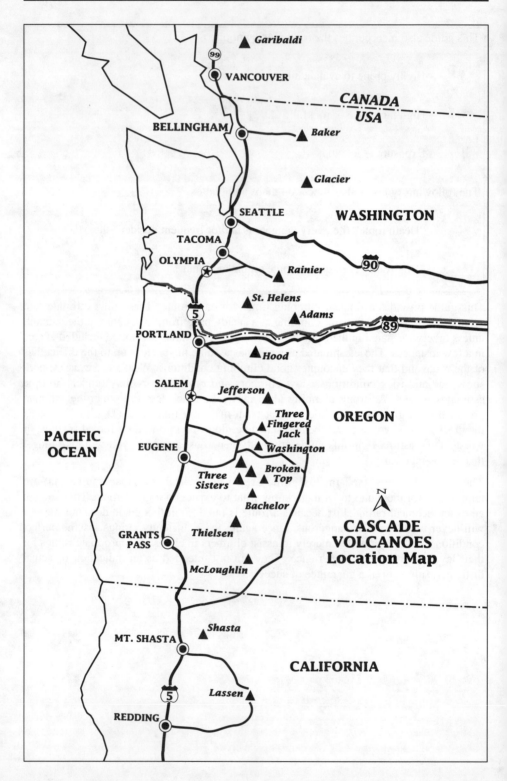

The Cascade Volcanoes

Of the mountains of the Cascade Range, the volcanoes are the youngest. Geologists estimate the age of the oldest of these volcanoes at about 750,000 to 1 million years. A volcano is, strictly speaking, merely the vent through which ash, gas and magma comes to the surface of the earth, along with the accumulation of erupted material. There are countless volcanic vents in the Cascade Range, including many cinder cones, plug domes, shield volcanoes and stratovolcanoes.

All but one of the peaks included in this guide are of the stratovolcano variety. Stratovolcanoes are composite volcanoes formed by various flows and ejections of differing materials occuring over a long span of time, intermittently erupting and building. Whereas shield volcanoes consist solely of liquid basaltic flows, stratovolcanoes combine various materials (e.g., andesite, dacite, rhyolite, ash, tuffs, basalt and pyroclastic materials) and build upward more rapidly by piling these varying materials upon each other. The result is a high, often uniformly-shaped mass of varying consistency – as you might get if you built your own backyard volcano by piling up loose sand and gravel over a foundation of mud, rock and cement.

Most volcano eruptions are comparatively mild, involving expulsion of steam and ash, but when a volcano is in an eruptive phase, anything can happen, from Mount Baker's steam emissions in the mid-1970s to Mount St. Helens' violent 1980 decapitation. Needless to say, during any period of activity, it is best to stay off the volcanoes – not only those erupting but their neighbors, too. Warming beneath glaciers triggers massive floods and mudslides, breaking glaciers apart. Earthquakes cause massive rockfalls, icefalls or avalanches. Ash clouds bring lightning and low visibility, not to mention searing heat and suffocation.

Based on data gleaned from the Mount St. Helens eruption cycle, geologists now feel confident they can predict a major eruption, or at least give accurate warning of a potential eruption. However, volcano eruption predictions are about as useful as weather predictions. A good rule to follow is: If your mountain is blowing steam and ash, stay home.

Sadly, Mounts Mazama and Tehama cannot be included in this guide. Both of these one-time giants suffered caldera collapses, the former resulting in Crater Lake and the latter reborn as the lateral plug dome of Lassen Peak. During their eruptive cycles, it is theorized these volcanoes rapidly expelled the contents of their magma chambers and, having lost their internal support, fell in on themselves.

Lassen is the only peak included in this guide that is not a stratovolcano. Lassen is a large plug dome, built of fast-cooling, viscous dacite, which plugged its vent before any lateral flows could occur. Lassen's 1915 eruption proves it is capable of violence and destruction equal to any stratovolcano, however.

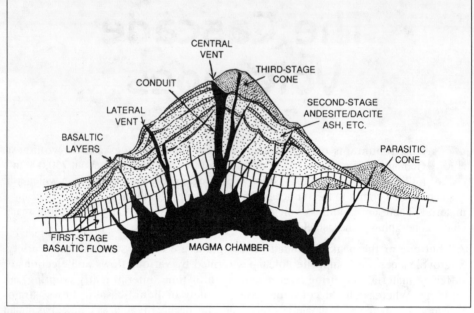

Conceptualized anatomy of a stratovolcano.

Native tribes witnessing volcanic activity on the peaks often interpreted eruptions as war-making amongst the spirits. Legends and myths have this mountain hurling rocks at that mountain, with one mountain spirit prevailing over another. Mounts Rainier, Mazama and Tehama all have had similar stories told of their heads being knocked off during fierce combat with other peaks. A well-known story is of a battle between Mounts Adams and Hood over Mount St. Helens, wherein the warriors showered each other with flaming rocks. Modern science has dispelled most myths about these fire mountains, although there are many unusual and creative modern myths, particularly about Mount Shasta.

There is little doubt that each of the volcanoes of the Cascade Range could erupt again someday, perhaps violently. Baker, Rainier, Hood and Shasta are very obviously still active volcanoes, as each has active vents, hot springs and "hot rocks." They are merely sleeping, and should by no means be pronounced dead.

A discussion of the volcanic history of each peak is included in later individual chapters. Those wishing to learn more about the geological history and composition of these volcanoes may consult the references listed in the bibliography. For climbers, it is usually enough to know that the rock on these peaks is rarely as stable as that of an average cairn.

Volcanic Rock

Some of the more challenging routes on Cascade volcanoes do have technical rock climbing sections, usually on unstable (i.e., rotten, crumbly, entirely untrustworthy) volcanic rock. Few climbers have anything good to say about it. Guidebook author Jeff

Cascade Volcanoes

Thomas described the rock on one Oregon volcano as having "the consistency of compacted graham crackers." Climber Ed Hall theorized: "The Oregon volcanoes are waiting to become Columbia River sandbars." He added, "Good rock is hard to find and, consequently, nontechnical routes can often be very hazardous due to rockfall or lack of secure hand and footholds." Technical routes are even more hazardous, for the very same reasons, on all of the Cascade volcanoes.

There is no truly high-quality rock climbing to be found on any volcano included in this guide, with the possible exception of recent bolted routes on Lassen Peak's newly discovered welded tuff. As a general safety rule, avoid volcanic rock whenever and however possible.

Glaciers

The volcanoes of the Pacific Northwest coast are home to the largest glaciers in the contiguous United States. Glaciers are formed when more snow accumulates during successive winters than melts away each summer. The resulting mass of snow builds up, compacts, and if there is sufficient slope and mass, is pulled down the mountainside by gravity. Glaciers are slow movers; objects lost in crevasses, including bodies of unfortunate climbers, are interred only to be revealed at the terminus decades, sometimes centuries, later.

Effects of glaciation on the Cascade volcanoes are obvious: glaciers have breached Mount Hood's and Glacier Peak's craters; worn away the soft slopes of Mounts Washington, Thielsen and Three Fingered Jack; and the Emmons and Winthrop Glaciers are undercutting their retaining ridges, resulting in mass wasting on an enormous scale. Glaciers pick up rock debris, which speeds up the erosive process. They are transporters of tons of material, pushing, swallowing or carrying mountain debris for a slow ride down the mountain.

The most important glacial features to climbers are crevasses. Crevasses are simply stress fractures in the ice, and represent the most common obstacle encountered on glaciers. Although glaciers are semi-flexible, and can "bend" over, around and through obstacles, they rarely do so without breaking. The more abrupt the turn or the greater the differential in glacier velocity, the more fractures will be formed. Crevasses most often form where the angle of descent (i.e., rate of descent) changes. If the angle is too severe, the glacier will likely break completely, sending huge chunks of ice avalanching down the peak and leaving "hanging" ice cliffs, such as those found atop Willis Wall on Mount Rainier and the Roman Headwall of Mount Baker. Undulations in the mountain's surface will cause an overriding glacier to buckle and crack. Glaciers squeezed through narrow corridors often shatter into nearly impassable, dangerous icefalls.

Negotiating crevasses can be very simple, but can also be very difficult. Lateral crevasses usually can be outflanked or crossed directly, depending upon length and width. Snow bridges sometimes offer a risky shortcut. Icefalls typically have seracs (ice towers) and jumbled crevasse patterns that are much more difficult and hazardous to pass. Bergschrunds sometimes cannot be passed at all. In winter, many crevasses are filled by snowfall and avalanches. Some are merely bridged by cornices and snowfall, traps to be sprung on unsuspecting climbers.

12 Cascade Volcanoes

Nearly every route in this guide involves glacier travel. Always rope up when traveling on glaciers, even when skiing. Just because you don't see crevasses and sinkholes doesn't mean they aren't there. Slips on glacial ice account for more climbing fatalities than falls into crevasses (although many "falls into crevasses" come at the end of a long, otherwise survivable slide), but hidden crevasses and sinkholes have swallowed up a great many unwary climbers. Being roped is not a guarantee you won't be injured or killed slipping on ice or falling into a crevasse, but it can greatly diminish that likelihood. First-aid training and crevasse rescue skills are important for every member of your climbing team, because if the only person in your party who knows these skills is the one dangling unconsious in a crevasse, he's in trouble!

Because this is not a climbing instruction book, no instruction on glacier travel or rescue techniques – other than the above warnings – is contained in this guide. Glacier travel and crevasse rescue techniques should be learned before attempting any glacier route.

Crevasses of the Park and Roosevelt Glaciers on Mount Baker.

Photo: Austin Post, U.S. Geological Survey

Cascade Volcanoes

Weather

Weather is not always poor in the Cascade range, even if it sometimes seems that way. The Pacific Northwest Coast's reputation for precipitation is not entirely unfounded, however. The lush rain forests of the Olympic Peninsula in Washington have the highest cumulative average rainfall in the nation. The slopes of Mount Rainier have seen world-record cumulative snowfalls.

In a nutshell, this is how Cascade mountain weather works: Warm, moist air blows in off the Pacific Ocean, squeezing moisture-laden clouds against the mountains. These clouds dump excessive rain on the western slopes of the mountains, then dissipate as they pass over the Cascade crest. This warm, moist marine air condenses and freezes very rapidly when it hits a glaciated volcano, which accounts for tremendous snowfall received each year by these peaks. Western slopes are often lush and heavily vegetated, while eastern slopes, protected by rainshadows, usually are less foliated.

It should be pointed out that weather on the high, glaciated peaks of the Cascades can be remarkably different than lowland weather. High volcanoes "create their own weather." Because they rise into the atmosphere, they show the effects of incoming weather patterns more dramatically than at lower elevations. Overall, the severity of the weather tends to increase as one moves north. Different weather patterns contribute to this phenomenon. Still, all of the Cascade volcanoes experience severe storms during each year, and these storms cannot always be predicted. Prepare yourself for the worst, including wind, rain and snow, no matter what the weatherman says.

On the larger peaks, particularly Mounts Rainier and Shasta, lenticular cloud caps frequently form on or near the summits, sometimes obscuring the upper slopes. These clouds are formed when expansive warm marine air impacts dense cold mountain air. The clouds are usually accompanied by very high winds and much moisture. Lenticular cloud caps sometimes disperse as quickly as they form, but more often they engulf a mountaintop in a raging storm, sometimes depositing several feet of snow over several hours. Although it may be disappointing to have turned back in the face of a lenticular cloud cap, it is better than having continued your ascent to find that a full-on storm has settled in, leaving you stranded high on the mountain in high winds and extreme avalanche conditions. Indeed, one of Mount Rainier's greatest survival stories – and one of its most needless tragedies – occured inside one such lenticular cloud. A father and son, who had come well-prepared, dug in when they were enveloped by the storm during their descent. They were rescued several days later, when the storm cleared, hungry but alive. Meanwhile, two experienced climbers set off from Camp Muir as the storm began to settle on the summit, and continued into the maelstrom, discounting warnings from guides and other climbers already descending the mountain because of the storm. Sadly, and needlessly, they perished.

Winter climbers should go prepared for the worst weather imaginable. Fierce storms, with high winds and high volumes of snowfall, often rage for several days on the high volcanoes, and can come without warning. Breaks between winter storms seldom last more than a few days. Plan winter climbs as you would a Himalayan expedition, because winter weather on the Pacific Northwest Coast isn't very much different than what you might find on Mount McKinley or Mount Everest.

Cascade Volcanoes

A lenticular cloud caps Mount Rainier.

Photo: Austin Post, U. S. Geological Survey

That weather changes can occur suddenly and dramatically is well-illustrated by a mining-era report of 100°-plus temperatures on the summit of Mount Adams in the afternoon, followed within 12 hours by a storm with minus 48° temperatures. Just because it is sunny and calm doesn't mean it won't soon be freezing and blustery.

The majority of weather-related problems occur when climbers are unable to find their way down out of a storm, or are trapped in a storm with no food or shelter. Whiteout conditions are frequent on all volcanoes, and are particularly problematic on featureless terrain, which means it is very easy to get lost in a whiteout on easier routes. Carry a compass and take bearings here and there along the way so you can more easily find your way down if the weather deteriorates. Don't descend by a different route unless you already know where it leads.

Of all considerations of mountain travel in the Cascades, weather should be among the foremost to climbers. Weather has been the culprit, directly or indirectly, in many climbing deaths on the Cascade volcanoes. Prepare for the worst no matter what the weather report says. Check weather forecasts and avalanche conditions before your climb. Although the weatherman is not always right about good weather, when it comes to poor weather, considering your life may be in the bargain, you should give him the benefit of the doubt.

Volcano Climbing

Why do we climb the volcanoes? The climbing is tedious, the terrain hazardous, the risks great. But the rewards – great views of a spectacular landscape and a "head-in-the-clouds" feeling – make reaching the summit unique and gratifying. For some people, "Because it's there," is probably as good a reason to climb as any. For others, climbing a high volcano is a test of courage, strength or endurance. For many others, it is simply to be able to point to the mountain from the lowlands and say, "I climbed it."

Whatever the motivation, all climbers need to be aware of volcano climbing's rigors and hazards, and how best to prepare for or avoid them.

Preparation

Climbers should be in good physical condition prior to attempting most of the routes included in this guide. A volcano climb typically only involves several long hours of trudging up a steady incline at altitude. Use this as a basic guideline: If you can't run 10 kilometers at an even pace without stopping, you shouldn't be climbing above 10,000 feet. You will slow your companions down and increase your chances of becoming fatigued, which can lead to an accident. Train for your climb (or climbing season) as you would for a marathon, because an ascent of a high volcano can be as strenuous if not more so. Whatever you do, don't make your companions drag you up the mountain because you aren't in shape (or down the mountain because you weren't). Consult your physician prior to starting any new exercise program, and get your doctor's permission before climbing if you have any health problems that may be affected by very strenuous activity.

Experience, or lack thereof, is often an important factor in mountaineering accidents. Inexperienced and unprepared climbers often make fatal mistakes; experienced climbers usually know better. Inexperienced climbers should not climb on glaciers or at high elevations, no matter how easy the terrain. If you have no previous mountaineering experience, you should take a climbing instruction course or go on a guided climb prior to attempting any of these routes on your own. Climb non-technical routes at first, gradually working up to more demanding routes as you gain technique, experience and knowledge of your abilities and limitations. Practice rock, ice, self-arrest and crevasse rescue techniques as often as possible so you know what to do when the time comes.

Climbing the Volcanoes

Climbers bivouac on Mount Rainier. Photo: Mark Dale

When To Climb

The timing of your climb should be determined by several factors, including weather, snow and glacier conditions, trail conditions, permit requirements, etc. For most of the Cascade volcanoes, climbing conditions are best from late May through July. Before (and sometimes during) June, snow and weather are less reliable, crevasse bridges collapse more easily, and trails and roads may still be snow-covered; after July, rockfall hazard increases, snow slopes become more icy, and crevasses open up and become difficult or impassable. It is a tradeoff as to whether you want a difficult approach but better climbing conditions, or an easy approach with worse climbing conditions. During years of heavy snowpack, July and August may offer the best overall climbing conditions. In years of light snowfall, May and June are often ideal for volcano climbing. This is not to say that climbing conditions will not be good during the rest of the year. Autumn is a popular season, although crevasses are wide open on many glaciers, which is a plus for timid souls afraid of plunging into a hidden crevasse, a minus for everyone else. Between October and April, climbs should be done only when weather and snow conditions are stable.

Routes on volcanic ridged and headwalls, which usually are rotten and subject to rockfall, should be attempted ony during certain weather conditions. Wait for a long cold spell, preferably following a snow or rainfall. This will help ensure that loose rocks will be frozen in place, reducing the risk of rockfall and avalanche and providing a more solid climbing surface.

Of course, this means that most ascents of the volcanoes are made during late May, June, July and early August, so you'll be fighting crowds for elbow room on the summit and possibly waiting in line along the way on the" dog" routes of some of these peaks.

This is all very generalized. Some routes require specific weather and snow conditions or else they are deadly; other routes are in shape all year except during poor weather or

Climbing the Volcanoes

avalanche conditions. If you seek solitude, schedule your climb between Monday and Friday. The more remote your objective, the less likely you will find other climbers en route. It really all depends upon what you want out of your climbing experience.

Clothing and Equipment

Climbers using this guide should already know what to bring and how to use it. For those who don't, the list that follows is a good starting point, but you should consult the references listed in this guide and take a mountaineering instruction course from a qualified guide service. *Mountaineering: The Freedom of the Hills* (The Mountaineers 1992) is perhaps the best overall comprehensive mountaineering instruction book available, containing instructions for nearly every aspect of mountain travel. However, once again, be warned that you can't learn how to climb by reading a book, even a good one. Take a climbing instruction course, complete a guided climb, do some easy glacier climbs and perfect belaying, crevasse rescue and ice-axe arrest techniques before trying to climb these mountains on your own.

> The National Park Service publishes a list of recommended clothing and equipment for all summit climbers on Mount Rainier. It is a comprehensive list, applicable to many volcano climbs, and is repeated verbatim here:
>
> - Full-frame crampons
> - Lug-soled boots
> - Wool clothing
> - Down clothing
> - Waterproof clothing
> - Hard hat
> - Rope (7/16 inch x 120 ft.)
> - Mittens and gloves
> - Ensolite pad
> - Flashlight
> - Map and compass
> - Rescue pulleys
> - Wands
> - Ice axe
> - Sunglasses/goggles
> - First-aid kit
> - Sunscreen
> - Food
> - Carabiners (2)
> - Sleeping bag
> - Prussik slings (3) or ascenders (2)
> - Headlamp
> - Pitons, ice screws
> - Stove and fuel
> - Tent

At a minimum, you should bring an ice axe and crampons on any volcano climb. Snow slopes can be treacherously icy. If steep snow, glacier travel or ice climbing will be encountered, a rope is also a recommended minimum.

It is recommended that you bring a small selection of ice screws on every route involving snow or ice travel, just in case they are needed. On more technical routes, bring more technical gear. This guide does not make specific gear recommendations. It is enough to say that climbers attempting technical routes should bring a comprehensive assortment of equipment appropriate for the task at hand and use good judgment in its use. This guide assumes you already know how and where to use your equipment, and that if you don't, you will learn before you go climbing. If you have never placed ice screws, you have no business climbing a route that may require their use. The same goes for any other route requiring the use of technical equipment. For that matter, if you don't have self-arrest, belay and crevasse rescue skills, you shouldn't be climbing on snow or glaciers.

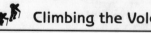 **Climbing the Volcanoes**

The point of bringing proper clothing is to keep yourself warm and dry in a hostile mountain environment. While it may seem possible to climb these peaks in shorts and a t-shirt on perfect, warm, windless days, there have been many hypothermia deaths attributed to casual or inadequate clothing. Dress properly and prepare for the worst; your life may depend on it.

Wear A Helmet!

Climbers attempting any route that passes over, beneath, near or through volcanic rock gullies and cliffs, and/or anywhere stonefall or icefall might occur, are advised to wear helmets. The rock on these peaks is mostly very poor, and can disintegrate with little provocation. Icicles and ice chunks regularly pelt climbers without warning. Helmets are recommended on all climbs, but mostly on those with potential for rock or ice fall. Granted, a helmet won't protect you from 2.6 million cubic yards of debris, but it might save your life if you get hit in the head by a more typical projectile.

Mountain Hazards

Mountaineering has numerous objective dangers, and routes described in this guide are not exceptions. Climbers venturing onto these mountains venture into a plethora of hazards. Despite all the obvious, potential hazards of mountaineering, thousands of ascents are made each year without incident or injury. However, climbers shouldn't be too smug, especially on the Cascade volcanoes. Even if you are very experienced and exercise perfect judgment, you may still get wiped out by an errant ice chunk. There are no guarantees of safety on these mountains, so proceed with caution and at your own risk.

Climbers negotiate a crevasse on Mount Shasta's Hotlum Glacier.

Photo: Michael Zanger, courtesy Shasta Mountain Guides

Climbing the Volcanoes   19

This guide makes an effort to point out obvious objective hazards. However, be aware that even if a route description does not have a warning of possible dangers, they may still exist. In June 1981, 11 climbers were killed in an unforeseen icefall on the Ingraham Glacier route on Mount Rainier, well illustrating that grave, unpredictable dangers lurk even on standard, non-technical routes. Changes in weather can turn a sunny afternoon snow hike into a semi-Himalayan expedition, or turn previously moderate snow slopes into icy death traps. Fatigued climbers can easily make a fatal misstep, particularly during the descent.

Warnings in this guide are intended to let climbers know of dangers that are frequently encountered on given routes. Avalanches and rockfall can occur at any time on almost any route in this guide. However, some routes have especially high frequencies of these events during certain conditions. The risk of falling into a crevasse is greatest in the late spring, when many crevasses are still covered but snow is melting rapidly, but people fall into crevasses throughout the year. Avalanche danger is highest after a snowfall, during high winds, and during mid-winter to late spring (in late spring, especially, masses of wet snow and cornices are regularly sloughed off by the mountains, posing a great threat to climbers and skiers alike), but even in late summer, avalanches can and do occur. Cornices and seracs regularly collapse and cause avalanches, so climbers should know how to spot and avoid them. Routes passing under ice cliffs obviously pose a greater threat of icefall than other routes, and climbing immediately after an avalanche is no guarantee that another isn't coming. Routes climbing over, through or around rock bands, in gullies, and on or under buttresses (which are usually very rotten and unstable), face an increased risk of rockfall. During winter and spring, and at unexpected times all year, storms envelop peaks in high winds and heavy snow. Winter climbers face an increased risk of frostbite, avalanche burial and of being trapped by a storm. Because of rapid changes in elevation during a very short time period (from sea level to 14,000 feet in less than 24 hours, in some cases), edema and acute mountain sickness can strike, but usually not without some warning. If you don't feel well and symptoms persist, you should retreat. This list of mountain hazards could go on and on. Hopefully, this summary has conveyed the idea that mountain climbing can be dangerous. To paraphrase Smokey the Bear, "Only you can prevent climbing accidents."

Unfortunately, no one can predict exactly which routes will be subject to rockfall, icefall, avalanches or other natural occurrences, and even the weatherman cannot always predict the coming of a major storm. Climbers should be wary of these dangers at all times, and avoid them whenever possible. To climb certain routes, however, one must be willing to face these risks. Once again, this guidebook is no substitute for good judgment or experience. Be sure you know what you are up against before you attempt any route. Check weather and avalanche conditions before each climb. Make sure you and your entire party have adequate experience and knowledge of the mountain and your chosen routes of ascent and descent.

It is apparent from the eruption of Mount St. Helens that volcanoes have great destructive potential, and climbers should be mindful of some of the effects of volcanic eruptions. Obviously, if the mountain you are climbing erupts, you are in serious trouble. However, the eruption of a neighboring volcano can create equally hazardous conditions. Lightning is an infrequent hazard, but lightning strikes are not uncommon on high volcanoes. During foul weather, stay off high points and ridges if possible; during a

Climbing the Volcanoes

storm, discard all metal objects until the storm has passed. Don't hide beneath trees or in caves, but out in the open, away from any potential conductor of electricity.

It is wise to check trail, weather, avalanche and climbing conditions by calling for information before your trip. Most Park Service and Forest Service district offices will gladly inform you of current conditions or special hazards.

If conditions become dangerous, for any reason, or you realize your chosen route is beyond your ability, don't be afraid to turn back. It is wiser to descend than to continue upward under questionable circumstances. You can come back another time. If you press on despite warning signs, you may not make it back. Your life is hopefully more important than reaching the summit of an icy heap of crumbly rocks. Think of it this way: There are thousands of mountains, but you have only one life.

Altitude Sickness

Altitude sickness is not an uncommon malady on the high volcanoes, particularly on Mounts Rainier and Shasta. Lowlanders, coming from sea level to over 10,000 feet in a 24-hour period without acclimatization, and in a rush to get to the summit and back before work on Monday, are particularly susceptible.

Symptoms include headache, dizziness, nausea, vomiting, weakness, shortness of breath, blueness of lips, chills, insomnia, increased pulse and respiration, blurred vision, confusion and disorientation. More serious symptoms include a tight chest, dry cough, noisy, "bubbling" breathing, rapid pulse, frothy or blood-tinged sputum, severe headache and convulsions. If you or any of your party experiences or exhibits any of these symptoms, descend immediately, slow down to reduce demand for oxygen, and breathe deeper and faster (this may cause nausea and dizziness, but keep at it). In severe cases, give oxygen if available. The sooner you get to lower elevation, the faster you will recover from mountain sickness.

Like almost any other mountain hazard, prevention is easier than treatment. Acclimatize, increase fluid intake and carbohydrate consumption, decrease fats in the diet, avoid alcohol prior to your climb, and don't smoke or take anti-depressants. Eating a big lunch on the summit of a high volcano can easily induce nausea. Don't be embarrased if you start puking on the summit of a volcano; you won't be the first. Just be sure to descend as quickly as is safe if you feel ill so nothing worse happens.

Hypothermia

Hypothermia is a genuine risk for all backcountry travelers, particularly volcano climbers. This often-fatal lowering of the body temperature is brought on by continued exposure to low temperatures, winds and rain – usually a combination of all three. These conditions are all too frequently present on the Cascade volcanoes. Climbers venturing too far from the safety and comfort of shelter with inadequate clothing risk hypothermia. Wool clothing and some synthetics, such as polypropylene, insulate even when wet, and are recommended. However, without a weather-resistant shell, any insulating clothing has limitations. Do everything possible to stay warm and dry, particularly during rainy and windy conditions.

Hypothermia's symptoms include fatigue, awkwardness, chills, lethargy, irritability, clumsiness, uncontrolled shivering and slurred speech. Most victims don't realize they are hypothermic. Act quickly to save them. Stop, find shelter (erect a tent or dig a snow

Climbing the Volcanoes 21

A climber descends Mount Baker's Coleman Glacier. Photo: Jeff Smoot

cave if you must), get the victim's wet clothes off and get him or her into a sleeping bag (with somebody undressed and warm if the victim appears seriously hypothermic, although decency permits you modest rescuers to wear underwear). If you can't stop where you are, get down fast! Warm liquids should be given to conscious victims, but not to comatose victims. If the victim does not appear to recover, send someone for help immediately. The faster the victim's body temperature is raised, the better his or her chances of survival.

Like altitude sickness, prevention of hypothermia is easier than the cure. If you suspect you or one of your partners is becoming hypothermic, get to shelter quickly.

Winter Climbing

Despite inherent hazards, winter ascents of the Cascade volcanoes are popular. Winter ascents sometimes can be made under perfect conditions with no more risk than a late-spring or late-fall ascent. More often, though, winter climbs involve climbing conditions akin to those in Anarctica.

The major considerations for winter climbing are weather and snow conditions. Cascade weather is unpredictable enough during the summer; during the winter, fierce storms lasting several days are not uncommon. Snowfall and high winds accompany these frigid storms, and whiteout conditions are frequent, particularly above timberline. Parties have become lost and pinned down for days by storms, and fatalities have occurred.

Climbing the Volcanoes

> The National Park Service recommends the following equipment for winter climbers on Mount Rainier (in addition to the list on page 17):
> - Extreme cold sleeping bag
> - Double boots
> - Expedition tent
> - Extra wands (200 minimum)
> - Two-way radio
> - Avalanche cords or beacons
> - Additional ropes
> - Down parka, pants, mitts
> - Snowshoes or skis
> - Snow shovel
> - Extra food and fuel (2 days)
> - Altimeter
> - Avalanche probes

Here are a few basic suggestions for winter climbing and avalanche avoidance:

• **Never climb alone!!**

• Check weather and avalanche conditions prior to every trip. Don't go out during poor weather or high avalanche danger. Avalanche hotline numbers are: British Columbia and Washington Cascades, (206) 526-6677; Oregon Cascades, (503) 326-2400; Mount Shasta, (916) 926-5555.

• Register with park or wilderness rangers prior to your climb, and give a good indication of what route you are climbing and when you are expected back.

• Never travel during or immediately after a snowstorm. How long to wait is an often-debated question; it is up to you and your better judgment.

• Carry avalanche cords (or better, avalanche transceivers), probe poles and a collapsible snow shovel on all winter climbs.

• Avoid soft, steep snow slopes, leeward slopes and obvious avalanche-prone slopes and gullies.

• Learn about avalanches and how to predict and avoid them. Also, learn avalanche search and rescue techniques before your climb. Be prepared for a search and rescue, just in case. This means every member of your party should carry probe poles, a snow shovel and an avalanche transceiver on all winter climbs.

• When crossing a suspect slope, expect to be buried, and prepare accordingly. Button up, put on mittens and a hat, loosen your pack and ski pole straps, and turn your avalanche transceiver to "transmit" mode (or tie into an avalanche cord). Only one person at a time should cross an avalanche slope, and everyone else should watch carefully.

• Climb above fracture lines and cornices, if possible.

• Potential avalanche paths should be used only if there is no other feasible route, and then only with extreme caution.

• When traveling above treeline in questionable weather, wand your route so you can find your way back if a storm sets in.

• Travel on ridgelines instead of open slopes whenever possible.

• Take enough food and fuel to last at least two extra days.

• Have someone at base camp in communication with the climbing party via two-way radio or cellular phone. This person can summon a rescue quickly if there is trouble.

Climbing the Volcanoes

Although foul weather is the major hazard for winter climbers, avalanches are more feared. Avalanches can range from minor snow sloughs to huge slabs capable of great damage. A high volume of snowfall, wind-accumulated snow, and rapidly changing weather patterns on the Cascade volcanoes account for particularly high avalanche danger at certain times. Warm, wet weather or a rapidly rising temperature with an accompanying wind are common warning signs of avalanche danger, and questionable snow slopes should be avoided during such weather. During unstable snow conditions, almost anything can trigger an avalanche. Be aware of shifts in wind direction, freezing rain and rising temperatures, and stay off unstable slopes. Climbers should have training and experience in spotting and avoiding dangerous avalanche conditions and should be familiar with avalanche rescue techniques before they venture onto these mountains, particularly in winter and spring. Avoiding potential avalanche slopes is the best way to avoid getting caught in an avalanche.

Frostbite is also a risk during winter and cold-weather ascents. Keeping your extremities warm, dry and unconstricted is important. Overly tight boots (which reduce circulation) and insufficient insulation of finger and toes make frostbite more likely.

Avalanche Survival and Rescue

If you are caught in an avalanche, do everything you can to stay on top of the sliding snow. Discard all equipment and begin "swimming" to keep atop the avalanche. This may keep you on the surface. If you can't stay on top, and are buried, close your mouth and eyes and cover your face with your arms. This will help create an airspace. As the snow stops sliding, try to enlarge your airspace before the snow solidifies, which is usually instantaneous. If you have time and if you can tell which way to dig (spit if you can't tell which way is up), dig furiously towards the surface. If you are lucky, you will

An ice avalanche cascades down Mount Rainier's Willis Wall.

Photo: Ashael Curtis, courtesy National Park Service

24 Climbing the Volcanoes

get an arm out and create an air hole, which may permit you to be found and rescued more quickly. If you can't get out, try to relax and wait. Conserve your air by staying calm and breathing slowly. Chances of survival are reduced by more than fifty percent after half an hour of burial, so the more you can do to conserve your precious air, the better your chances of survival. Because of avalanche danger alone, it is very unwise to climb by yourself in winter and spring. Parties of three are a recommended minimum for safety.

If a companion is buried in an avalanche, don't panic! Watch and make note of the last place you saw the victim. After making sure all surviving members of your group are safe, make a visual search of the entire avalanche area for clues. This is where avalanche transceivers come in handy. Mark areas where you last saw the victim, and begin your search. If you can't locate anything, start probing in accumulation areas first, using an avalanche probe, ski pole or ice axe, in that order or preference, as avalanche victims are buried 4´ feet deep, on average. Be careful, but be fast! Don't stop looking until help arrives. If you are the only person around, you are the victim's only chance for survival. Unless reliable help is less than 15 minutes away, you must do your best to find the victim immediately.

Reading an avalanche book and taking an avalanche safety course are good ideas before you venture into the Cascade Range during winter.

Four levels of avalanche danger are usually given by reporting agencies:

Low Hazard: Mostly stable snow exists and avalanches are unlikely (but still possible), except in isolated pockets on steep snow-covered open slopes and gullies. Backcountry travel is generally safe in areas with low hazard.

Moderate Hazard: Areas of unstable snow exist and avalanches are possible on steep snow-covered open slopes and gullies. Backcountry travelers should use caution in areas with moderate hazard.

High Hazard: Mostly unstable snow exists and avalanches are likely on steep snow-covered open slopes and gullies. Backcountry travel is not recommended except in avalanche-free areas.

Extreme Hazard: Widespread areas of unstable snow exist and avalanches are certain on steep snow-covered open slopes and gullies. Backcountry travel is not recommended except in avalanche-free areas. Backcountry travel should be avoided. (Even auto travel should be avoided, if possible.)

Just as this guide cannot provide mountaineering instruction, it also cannot provide a thorough lesson on avalanche safety, snow travel, navigation or winter mountaineering survival strategies. Winter climbers should learn about preventing frostbite and hypothermia and avalanche prediction and rescue, and should know how to prepare for winter travel before they find themselves lost in a blizzard or buried in wet snow.

Ski Mountaineering

Ski ascents and descents of Cascade volcanoes have become popular. During winter and spring, skis often are necessary to approach the volcanoes. Some volcano routes can be ascended pretty easily by experienced, properly equipped skiers. Skiing offers a much faster means of descent for those who have mastered the necessary skills, but it does have additional risks for those who have not. Volcano skiing has lately become an end in itself rather than merely a means of descent. Many glaciers offer thrilling downhill runs of many thousands of feet – even miles – but with all attendant risks of glacier travel amplified by the dynamics and speed of skiing. Glacier Peak, Mount Baker, Mount Rainier, Mount Adams, Mount Shasta and Mount Hood have all been climbed on skis. Skiers have descended most of the less-technical routes on the volcanoes, and even such routes as the Nisqually Icefall and Liberty Ridge on Mount Rainier and the Newton Clark Glacier Headwall on Mount Hood. Snowboarders have descended from the summits of several of these peaks, by various routes, and no doubt will continue to do so as this sport increases in popularity. Skiers and snowboarders now vie for the season's first descent of such peaks as Rainier, Hood and Shasta.

If you plan on making a ski descent, remember to rope up on glaciers. Skiing can cut your descent time greatly, turning a three-hour trudge into a joyful 20-minute run. But, at speed, you might not see a crevasse until you are plunging into it.

Extreme ski mountaineering's risks are very great. Those with proper experience, equipment and conditioning for ski mountaineering (not to mention a good dose of fortitude) may proceed and enjoy; like climbers, those without are cautioned to get proper experience, equipment and conditioning before they endanger themselves foolishly.

A skier crosses the Garibaldi Névé.

Photo: Mark Dale

Climbing the Volcanoes

No-Trace Ethics

Because of the popularity of the Cascade volcanoes, many well-known trails, campsites and climbing routes are showing signs of overuse. No-trace use of the wilderness areas of the Cascade Range is urged by the National Park Service and U.S. Forest Service.

> Here are some simple suggestions to help minimize your impact on the mountain environment:
>
> - Travel in small groups to do less damage to meadows and campsites.
>
> - Use a stove for cooking, and bring a tent rather than relying on scarce natural resources. Campfires are not permitted in most wilderness areas in Washington, Oregon and California.
>
> - Use pit toilets or practice accepted human waste disposal practices (including not eliminating near water sources, and/or packing it out in plastic bags).
>
> - Plan your actions so as to make the least impact on the environment.
>
> - Stay on trails, even when muddy, to avoid sidecutting or erosion. Don't take shortcuts on switchbacks.
>
> - Tread gently on vegetation, which is often fragile on high mountain slopes.
>
> - Hike on snow or talus whenever possible, rather than causing unnecessary erosion on pumice slopes and vegetation.
>
> - Choose stable sites for camps and rest stops, avoiding fragile vegetation.
>
> - Use existing campsites rather than creating new ones.
>
> - Camp on snow instead of bare ground whenever possible.
>
> - Don't construct rock windbreaks or clear bare-ground areas of rocks or vegetation for any reason.
>
> - Avoiding having leftover food, so as not to attract wildlife to your camp.
>
> - Don't bring your pets with you.
>
> - Pack out your trash.

Litter and human waste disposal are major problems on many of the Cascade volcanoes. On Mount Rainier, the Park Service hands out plastic bags for human waste disposal. Putting any refuse into crevasses, or burying it in snow or soil or under rocks is not acceptable. Use pit toilets and trash containers where available, or else pack it out, particularly in high-use areas. If you are on a remote, infrequently-traveled route, you might be okay leaving your byproduct out in the open, where wind and sun will decompose it. But on crowded routes, where your rope might drag through it, it is best to use a well-sealed plastic bag to take it where it can be disposed of properly.

Climbing the Volcanoes

Wilderness Permit Requirements

Many of the wilderness areas included in this guide have established quotas on the number of persons who may occupy certain campsites and climb certain routes. Permit systems have been implemented at many wilderness areas. These measures, though occasionally restrictive, are meant to help reduce the harm humans have caused and continue to cause in these fragile mountain environments. Park Service and Forest Service Wilderness Management Plans have established "limits of acceptable change" for certain high-use areas. When an area exceeds the limits of acceptable change, access is often restricted. Examples of areas where human use has had significant adverse impact are Lake Helen on Mount Shasta, Jefferson Park on Mount Jefferson, Green Lakes, the South Sister Climbers' Trail, and Camps Muir, Schurman and Hazard on Mount Rainier, to name a few. The more popular the corridor of travel, the more likely it will be overused and abused, not only by climbers but by other wilderness visitors as well.

Climbers are not any better or worse than the majority of other wilderness users with regard to most overuse issues, but we can help dispel any conception that climbers are less inclined to be concerned with human impacts by spreading out onto less-traveled routes and into areas where adverse impacts are less severe, and doing what we can to lessen our impact in sensitive areas. When you have climbed the standard non-technical route on Mount Shasta, for example, turn your attention to the other routes on the mountain. The fewer trips up heavily-impacted routes, the less likely future restrictions will be imposed.

Permit systems and overnight quotas are usually implemented to relieve the burden wilderness users have imposed upon the mountains. A good way to ensure permit availability – and some solitude – is to come during the work week, when the mountains are nearly empty of human visitors, rather than on weekends, when they are packed full. Campsites crowded on Saturday night are usually vacant on Tuesday and Wednesday nights. Specific wilderness and National Park regulations (including permits and quotas) will be discussed where appropriate in the following chapters. Please do your best to follow these regulations, and do what you can to minimize your impact.

Although we won't likely wear the mountains down with our boot soles, we may greatly detract from the beauty and serenity of the mountain environment unless we think and act in ways appropriate to preserving our wilderness areas.

To Report Climbing Accidents

To report a climbing accident or other emergency, dial 911. Finding a phone can be difficult in some areas. Campers sometimes have CB radios, so if a phone is far away, stop at Forest Service campgrounds along the way and ask for help. If you cannot contact a 911 operator, dial "0" and ask for the emergency dispatch operator or county sheriff. The county sheriff is responsible for coordinating mountain rescue operations in most areas, except in national parks and some wilderness areas.

Mount Garibaldi

Atwell Peak, a sub-peak of Mount Garibaldi, from Dalton Dome. Photo: Don Serl.

Chapter One:
Mount Garibaldi
British Columbia (8,787 ft./2678m)

The northernmost volcano included in this guide is British Columbia's Mount Garibaldi. Strictly speaking, Garibaldi is not part of the Cascade Range proper, but instead is part of the Coast Mountains of British Columbia, as it lies well north of the Fraser River, the customary dividing line between the two ranges. However, in *Fire and Ice,* Stephen Harris noted that "Garibaldi and other volcanoes in the Coast Mountains may be structurally related (to the Cascade volcanoes) and represent a northern extension of the same geologic system." It is a "Cascade volcano" in this guide because, geologically speaking, Garibaldi is definitely part of the Cascade volcanic chain which, in fact, extends further north through Mounts Cayley and Meager to peaks in the southwestern Waddington Range and near Mount Silverthrone.

One of the lowest of the Pacific Coast stratovolcanoes, Garibaldi is neither the highest peak in Garibaldi Provincial Park, nor the highest volcanic peak in Canada (that honor going to Mount Edziza, 9,144 ft./2787m, in northwestern British Columbia). However, it stands out, alone, in the typical manner of Cascade volcanoes, whereas most other Canadian volcanic peaks are hidden within higher ranges of British Columbia. It is a singular, striking mountain, centerpiece of one of British Columbia's finest Provincial Parks.

Garibaldi, one of the youngest Pacific Rim volcanoes, has the distinction of being the only volcano in this guide that erupted through a glacial ice sheet. According to available evidence, Garibaldi once was partially supported by an ice age glacier. The wasting of the ice, it is theorized, caused the summit cone to collapse towards the west. This collapse would certainly explain Garibaldi's entirely untrustworthy rock. Ridges and faces are shattered, and rocks regularly rumble down the mountain's flanks without apparent provocation. Because Mount Garibaldi is composed of unstable rock, routes keep mostly to the glaciers and snow slopes, which are abundant in winter and spring, but which become "boggy" in late spring and usually vanish after June or July of most years. After the snow melts, crevasses and bergschrunds can pose difficulty and danger, and rockfall is always a hazard. For this reason, early season, cold-weather ascents are recommended for most routes up Garibaldi, and technical rock climbing is pretty much out of the question.

Mount Garibaldi was first ascended in 1907 by a mob (A. Dalton, W. Dalton, Atwell King, T. Pattison, J. Trorey and G. Warren). Its first winter ascent came in 1943, also by a crowd (Vernon Brink, R. McLellan, H. Parliament, J. Rattenburg and F. Roots). Garibaldi has three distinct summits: Garibaldi, the true summit, Dalton Dome (8,638

Mount Garibaldi

ft./2633m), a dome-like shoulder to the west, and Atwell Peak (8,596 ft./2620m), a pointed summit on the southwest (also known as Diamond Head). Its eastern flank is smothered by the Garibaldi Névé, a broad glacial sheet containing at least ten individually-named glaciers. The névé is a popular ski destination, particularly in spring, and provides open access to many climbing routes until late summer. Winter ski camping on the névé is common, but high winds are not uncommon, so most winter skiers and climbers wisely protect campsites by digging into the snow or constructing snow walls or igloos for shelter.

Winter ascents of Garibaldi are reasonably popular, which is likely due to the very loose nature of the volcano's rock. However, Garibaldi's routes can have high avalanche danger in winter and spring. It's a trade-off, depending on whether you prefer rockfall or avalanches. Ideal climbing conditions on Garibaldi can occur anytime during the winter (December to March), although ascents of less rockfall-prone routes are routinely made well into the summer. One should wait for a very cold spell following a brief warming period. With stable weather under such conditions, snow has settled, rocks are frozen in place, snow and ice offer secure climbing, crevasses are covered and avalanche danger is low. Such conditions occur once or twice (three times at most) during most winters in the Coast Mountains, so good luck trying to plan for them! When such conditions arrive, you must pack and go instantly – the good weather probably won't last long. Otherwise, wait until summer, when weather is more reliable, and take your chances with loose rock and crevasses.

Winter and early-season climbing parties commonly approach on skis; in late season, skiing across the névé is possible but not much easier than walking. By June or July, when most ascents are made, skis are rarely used.

For more information on routes not fully described in this guide, please refer to Bruce Fairley's *Climbing and Hiking in Southwestern British Columbia* (Gordon Soules Book Publishers, 1986).

All amenities are available in nearby Squamish. For additional information, contact:

    Squamish Forest District   (604) 898-2100
    42000 Loggers Lane
    Squamish, B.C. V0N 3G0

    Garibaldi/Sunshine Coast District, Box 220   (604) 898-3678
    Brackendale, B.C. V0N 1H0

To report a climbing accident or other emergency, call the Royal Canadian Mounted Police at (604) 892-9111.

Mount Garibaldi 31

Rating details appear on pages 4 through 7 of the Introduction.

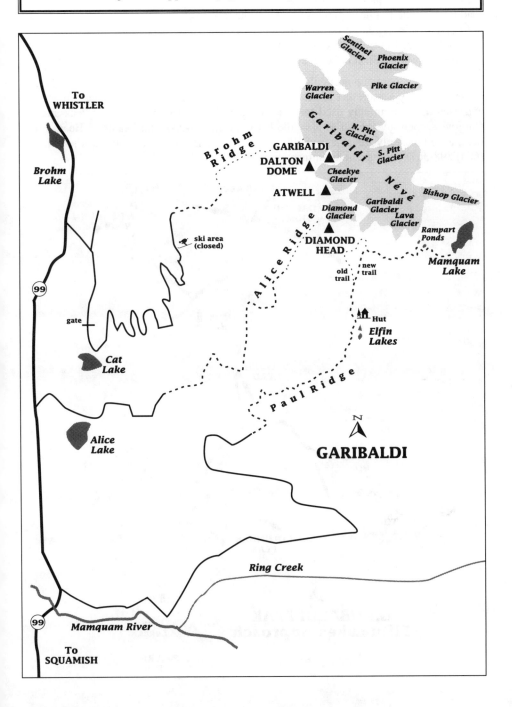

Mount Garibaldi

Elfin Lakes Approach

Garibaldi and Atwell's southern routes are commonly approached from Elfin Lakes via Paul Ridge Trail. To reach Paul Ridge Trail, turn off Provincial Highway 99 about 2.5 mi/4 km north of Squamish onto Mamquam Road. A 10 mi/16 km drive up a good gravel road leads to the trailhead parking lot. Hike the trail over Paul Ridge to Elfin Lakes (the hut currently is available on a first-come, first-in basis for a nightly fee of $10 per person, $25 per family, subject to change without notice). In winter, a marked ski route may be followed to Elfin Lakes Hut to avoid avalanche danger on the trail.

From the lakes, continue north along the trail to cairns that mark the way to the névé. In winter and early season this is avalanche-prone; in case of severe avalanche danger, the approach most-commonly used traverses over the gap between Columnar Peak and the Gargoyles, then goes north to a saddle between these peaks and Diamond Head. From here, a northeasterly traverse joins the former route. If you plan to stay in the hut, call (604) 898-3678 for current hut information.

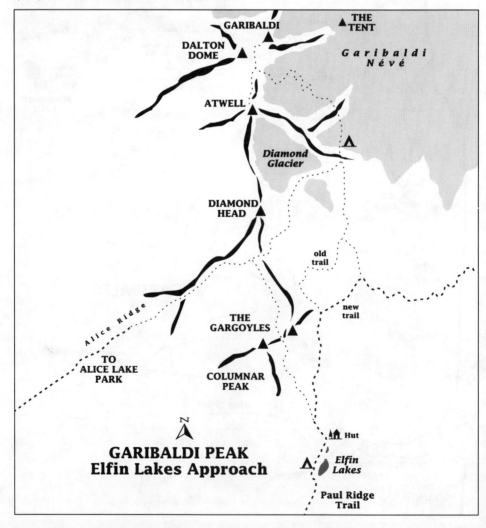

Mount Garibaldi

Alice Ridge Approach

Signs lead from Highway 99 to Alice Park, from which jeep roads lead up switchbacks onto Alice Ridge. A trail takes you to the saddle between Diamond Head and the Gargoyles. From here, continue northeast, as for Elfin Lakes approach, traversing onto the névé. Some parties bivouac at the saddle dividing Diamond Head from the Gargoyles.

Brohm Ridge Approach

An unmarked road leaves Highway 99 north of the Alice Park turnoff, just before Brohm Lake is reached. The road curves back south and up to Cat Lake. You'll reach a gate at 3 mi/4.8 km, just past a fork. The gate is locked at 5 p.m. on Friday evenings and not reopened until Sunday evening. After 5 p.m. Friday, the gatekeeper will let you out but not in (except in an emergency). So, if you want to drive in for a weekend ascent, come early on or before Friday. Otherwise, walk from the gate (a last resort), or try the tougher Brohm Ridge jeep road. If you get past the gate in time, continue up the rough road as far as you can make it. The road passes an abandoned ski area. From road's end, hike up Brohm Ridge to the névé. Camping is found at the cabin (about halfway along Brohm Ridge), or anywhere on the névé. In winter, this area is heavily used by snowmobilers.

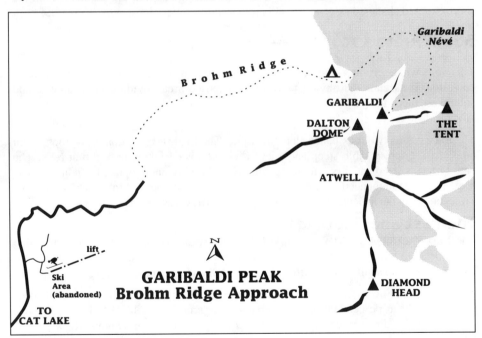

GARIBALDI PEAK — Brohm Ridge Approach

Atwell Peak
8,569 ft./2620m

Atwell Peak is the southwest summit of Garibaldi, and is sometimes called "Diamond Head." The summit was first reached by A. Armistead, Basil Darling, J. Davies, Frank Hewton and Allan Morkill in 1911. Early-season ascents are recommended so snow and ice can be climbed instead of loose rock. Atwell's ridges are sharp and exposed, its faces steep, loose and avalanche-prone, and its summit quite rotten. Still, it is a popular ascent, particularly in winter and early spring. Climbing Atwell is not recommended without snow or ice covering the rocks. Helmets are highly recommended.

North Ridge 6-8 hrs

This, the standard route, climbs the short north ridge of Atwell Peak from the Garibaldi-Atwell saddle. The common approach is via Elfin Lakes and Garibaldi Névé, although Alice Ridge is an equally feasible approach. Cross the névé and ascend toward the saddle, staying left of "The Tent" (a popular winter ski destination). Crevasses in the icefall are sometimes difficult to pass, and there is avalanche danger. From the saddle, ascend the short, exposed shattered ridge to Atwell's rotten summit. Very loose rock (Class 4).

South Arête   6-8 hrs

This somewhat serious route has gained popularity as a winter ascent, when it is in condition. It ascends the obvious and highly-exposed arête dividing the southeast and southwest faces directly to Atwell's summit pinnacle. Approach from Elfin Lakes or Alice Ridge.

The route passes two rock bands along the ridge. The final steep section of the route often consists of unprotectable steep snow and rime ice over frighteningly rotten rock. The entire route is steep and airy, providing enjoyable climbing under optimal conditions. The route is not recommended after early spring, although it has been climbed as late as June. Protection may be difficult or untrustworthy. Grade III, Class 4 or 5.

The East and Southeast Faces

The **East Face** of Atwell (3; 6-8 hrs) lies between the saddle and the southeast ridge and appears to have a feasible route, which would involve steep snow or ice and an exit gully to either the southeast or north ridge. Rockfall and avalanche hazard.

The **Southeast Face** (3; 6-8 hrs) is characterized by several couloirs (at least two of which have been descended on skis) separated by crumbling ribs. The leftmost major couloir offers a direct route to a point immediately north of the summit. Rockfall and avalanche hazard.

Northwest Face

This 1000m face has two routes, and possibilities for a few others, but high avalanche and rockfall danger make it an unwise choice except in perfect winter conditions. The face is approached from Brohm Ridge below the western flanks of Dalton Dome. From the head of Brohm Ridge, traverse south around the southeast ridge of Dalton Dome.

Mount Garibaldi

Mount Garibaldi from the southwest. Photo: Wally Kerchum

The **Siberian Express** route (④; 16 hrs) climbs the huge central couloir that leads up the northwest face to the notch just north of Atwell's summit. Rockfall, avalanche and icefall hazard. Grade V.

The **Armenian Express** (④; 16 hrs; rockfall, avalanche and icefall danger) climbs a narrow couloir just right of Siberian Express. A summit bivouac was required on the first ascent. Follow the couloir until loose rock forces a traverse onto the south ridge just below the summit. Grade V.

Atwell Peak as seen from Mount Garibaldi. Photo: Don Serl

Garibaldi Summit
8,787 ft./2678m

Garibaldi is the true summit, a rocky horn situated a bit north of Atwell and northeast of Dalton Dome. Two routes are commonly used, although it can be reached directly from either other summit. The East Face is most conveniently approached from Alice Ridge or Elfin Lakes and the Northeast Face from Brohm Ridge, but it is straightforward to cross below The Tent to get from one route to the other.

East Face 6-8 hrs

From Garibaldi Névé, ascend to the Garibaldi-Atwell saddle, then up the small Cheekye Glacier between Dalton Dome and Garibaldi. An easy ledge and short couloir on the west side lead to the northwest ridge and the summit. The portion of this route leading to the saddle may be quite crevassed in late season, and sometimes has high avalanche danger. There is some loose rock scrambling on the final pitch, with attendant rockfall hazard. Class 2.

Northeast Face/Warren Glacier ★ 6-8 hrs

This was the first-ascent route. Cross the Warren Glacier and climb to the Garibaldi Névé, then continue up to the headwall. Passing the bergschrund may be difficult, and often involves outflanking via the rotten ridges to the east or north. Once beyond that obstacle, either ascend broken rock or continue up the snow face to the summit. Class 3.

A view of Garibaldi Névé and Warren Glacier.   Photo: Don Serl

Mount Garibaldi

Dalton Dome
8,638 ft./2633m

Dalton Dome is the blunt summit southwest of Garibaldi summit. Its first ascent was made by the 1907 mob. It is best climbed from Garibaldi-Atwell saddle.

Dalton Dome Routes

The **North Face** route (④; 8-10 hrs) is approached from the end of Brohm Road. Ascend Brohm Ridge east onto the Warren Glacier. Ascend the Warren Glacier headwall on the far right, crossing the bergschrund to shattered rock, then continue up steep snow to a slight rib that gains the northwest shoulder. Continue up the ridge to the summit. This route features remarkably unstable rock. Grade III, Class 4 or 5. Rockfall and avalanche danger.

The **Northwest Face – Shoulder** route (③; 6-8 hrs) ascends the face right of the end of Brohm Ridge and, after moderate snow and poor rock climbing, joins the North Face route to the summit. Grade III, Class 4 or 5. Rockfall hazard.

The **Southwest Ridge** route (③; 8-10 hrs) follows the obvious stepped ridge that descends southwest from Dalton Dome. Grade III, Class 4. Rockfall, avalanche and icefall hazard.

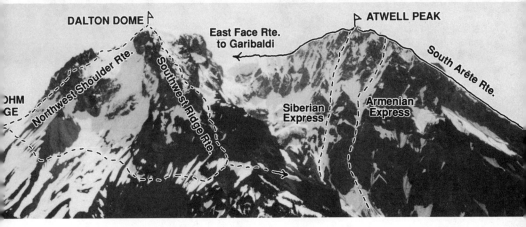

Dalton Dome and Atwell Peak as seen from the west. Photo by Don Serl.

Mount Baker

Mount Baker towers above Bellingham and Bellingham Bay. Taken from Lummi Indian Reservation.
Photo: Tim Boyer/Mountain Ski Adventures

Chapter Two:
Mount Baker
Washington, 10,778 ft./3285m

Mount Baker, the "northern sentinel" of the Cascade Range, is one of the iciest of the Cascade volcanoes, with 44 square miles of ice spread out among its 12 glaciers (by comparison, Mount Rainier has only 35 square miles of ice). Rising a short distance south of the Canadian border, only about 50 miles from Bellingham Bay, and a few miles south of the 49th Parallel, Mount Baker is a dominating presence from any northern Puget Sound vantage. Its stark white glaciers are clearly visible from Seattle, and on a clear day you can see it from Mount Rainier, more than 100 miles away.

Mount Baker was "discovered" in 1792 by Captain Vancouver's first mate, Joseph Baker, for whom it was named. On that voyage, Baker had claimed the first ascent of Hawaii's giant volcano, Mauna Kea, but apparently did not consider climbing Baker. Juan de Fuca may have sighted the peak in 1592. The first recorded mention of the mountain was in 1790 by Manuel Quimper, a Spanish navigator, who named it "La Gran Montaña de Carmelo." Long before Quimper or Baker's sightings, local Nooksack tribesmen and other indigenous people knew the mountain as "Koma-Kulshan" (meaning "Wounded Mountain" or "Damaged Mountain" or "Steep White Mountain" or "White Shining Mountain" or "Great White Watcher," or any of several other translations depending upon your reference). A native legend had it that an angry god struck the mountain with a lightning bolt, wounding or breaking the great peak, causing it to "bleed" molten rock, undoubtedly the best explanation of a volcanic event that could be mustered by the superstitious inhabitants of the mountain's foothills.

Mount Baker volcano was active during the mid-1970s, when Sherman Crater broke open and began spewing steam and ash clouds — minor compared with Mount St. Helens in 1980, but of great concern to local residents, particularly those living below Baker Lake. The peak has settled down a bit, but seismic activity beneath the mountain continues. Thermal vents in the vicinity of the peak have been considered as a source of geothermal energy. Obviously, Mount Baker is not finished. There is little doubt among geologists that it could erupt again in the not-too-distant future. The mountain was supposedly more precipitous prior to the mid-1800's, but a summit "slump" or partial collapse is thought by some geologists to have occurred (the result of some kind of seismic activity within the mountain), giving Grant Peak its more rounded appearance. Like other volcanos in this guide, Mount Baker's rock is bad if not worse, and Mount Baker's flanks are slowly becoming moraines and sand bars. Among Mount Baker's sub-summits are Sherman Peak, a sharp point rising directly above the Sherman Crater, and the Black Buttes, known individually as Colfax Peak (the east butte, nearest the summit)

Mount Baker

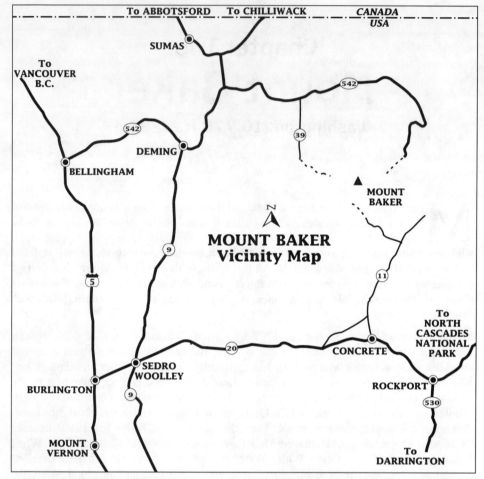

and Lincoln Peak, standing as crumbly remains of a former crater rim of Mount Baker; the Deming Glacier now occupies that obstructed vent. There are routes to the summits of the Black Buttes, but none is recommended.

Mount Baker was first climbed in 1868 by Edmund T. Coleman, David Ogilvy, Thomas Stratton and John Tennant. Coleman, an English librarian living in Victoria, B.C., had made two previous attempts to climb the mountain, and was devoted to the task. His detailed journals and artworks provide a remarkable glimpse of early climbing attempts on Mount Baker. Coleman also was a member of Mount Rainier's first ascent party, but did not complete the ascent with Hazard and Van Trump.

Of further historical interest were the Mount Baker "marathons," which began in 1911 and ended in 1913. The marathons were essentially a race from Bellingham to the summit of Mount Baker and back to Bellingham, involving car or train travel and many miles of trail running. After one contestant fell into a crevasse, and due to growing fear of a worse accident, the event was discontinued. The Mount Baker Marathon has been revived as the modern Ski-to-Sea Race, which begins at the Mount Baker ski area, and

Mount Baker

involves downhill and cross-country skiing, running, bicycling, canoeing or kayaking, and sailing to Marine Park in Bellingham.

Climbers should be particularly wary of crevasses on Mount Baker, which seems to have more than any other Cascade volcano. Hidden crevasses swallow up dozens of climbers each year; luckily, most are pulled out without serious injury. Early-season climbers especially should beware of crevasses, even if none are visible. Even in late season, crevasses can surprise you. Amazingly, considering all of the people who had climbed Mount Baker unroped prior to that year, the first known crevasse-related death on Mount Baker occurred in 1913.

Because Mount Baker receives an annual average of over 50 feet of snow, avalanches are also a very real danger, even on gentle slopes and during the summer months. This danger is compounded by warm, wet weather, which allows heavy snow to accumulate. Snow followed by warm, rainy weather (common on Mount Baker) spells certain avalanche conditions. A July 1939 avalanche high on the Deming Glacier killed six people, an event repeated more than once since. The volume of snowfall alone is a fair indicator that Mount Baker has very poor climbing weather during much of the year. In winter, it bears the brunt of arctic air masses, and the collision of these frigid masses with marine air blowing north up Puget Sound is responsible for the high winds, storms, clouds and snowfall common to the mountain. A winter ascent of Mount Baker can therefore be a very serious undertaking. Of course, the high snow accumulation feeds the glaciers and keeps the mountain white all year, and makes it a very attactive ski climb.

In 1984, 132,200 acres were added to the National Wilderness System, creating Mount Baker Wilderness. As a wilderness within the definition of the Wilderness Act of 1964, no motorized travel is permitted (except for a pie-wedge portion of the Easton Glacier – a privilege occasionally abused by snowmobilers who cross the saddle onto the Coleman Glacier). This has preserved Mount Baker's immediate slopes from the threat of logging and other commercial exploitation, and is a long-overdue tribute to a beautiful mountain. Permits may soon be required for entry into Mount Baker Wilderness. An advisory board composed of hikers, climbers and other wilderness users is reviewing access issues and, as with most other wilderness areas in the Cascade Range, permits are a near certainty. At time of publication, however, nothing was definite.

For more information about routes not thoroughly described in this guide, please refer to the *Cascade Alpine Guide Vol. 3* by Fred Beckey (The Mountaineers, 1981).

For current information about permits or access, contact:	
Mt. Baker Ranger District 2105 Highway 20 Sedro Woolley, WA 98284	(206) 856-5700
Glacier Public Service Center	(206) 599-2714
Supervisor's Office Mt. Baker-Snoqualmie National Forest 915 Second Avenue, Room 442 Seattle, WA 98174	(206) 442-0170

Mount Baker

Rating details appear on pages 4 through 7 of the Introduction.

Mount Baker Trail Approach

Mount Baker Trail 677 is commonly used to approach the north side routes. Turn south on Forest Service Road 39 from State Highway 542, (this is about one mile past the Glacier Public Service Center). The trailhead is on the left about eight miles up Road 39, just past the point at which the road changes from pavement to gravel. Two miles of hiking lead to the former site of Kulshan Cabin, at timberline. The cabin was torn down shortly after the area was granted wilderness status. The Coleman Glacier is just above, and provides access to the routes. In early season, it may be difficult to tell when you have reached the glacier. Alternatively, you can hike cross-country directly up Heliotrope Ridge to the lowest western point of the glacier; this route has fewer crevasse difficulties, but is less obvious and less-frequently used.

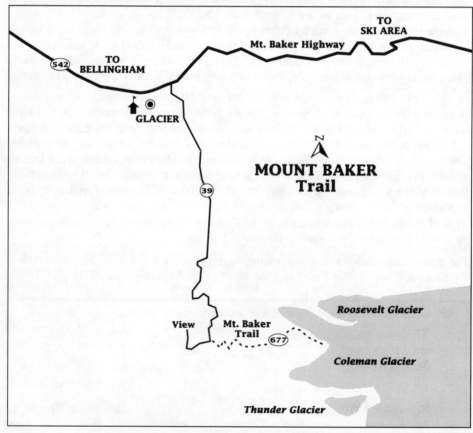

Mount Baker 43

Coleman – Upper Deming Glacier ★ ② 6-8 hrs

This was the approximate line of the original route climbed on Mount Baker in 1868 by Edmund Coleman and party, and remains the most popular route to the summit of Mount Baker. The route is approached via the Mount Baker Trail. From the cabin site, continue up the trail about .5 mile, and take a right up the "Hog's Back," a lateral moraine. At about 6,000 feet, you reach the glacier. It is possible to camp where Kulshan Cabin used to be, a nice flat spot that is too low for most parties except on crowded weekends. Most parties camp either at the top of the Hog's Back (also often crowded), or below the Black Buttes at about 9,000 feet on the Coleman Glacier (popular with small, unguided parties).

Ascend the right flank of the glacier (there are usually fewer crevasses farther west), then bear toward and beneath the Black Buttes to the saddle between Colfax Peak and Grant Peak. From the saddle, proceed upward via a pumice ridge, staying right of the "Roman Wall," and continue straight up, bearing right near the summit.

Beware of hidden crevasses, and stay roped on the descent. The Roman Wall has avalanched several times even in late season, so beware. Bombardment from the Black Buttes is an occasional hazard.

Baker Pass Trail Approach

Baker Pass Trail 603 is commonly used to approach the Easton Glacier route. From State Highway 20, drive north on Baker Lake-Grandy Lake Road (about 14 miles from either Sedro Woolley or Rockport). After about 12 miles, the road splits; take unpaved Forest

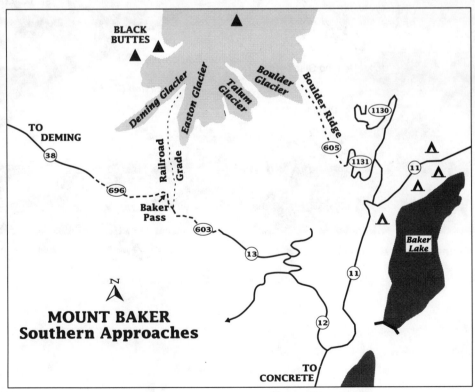

MOUNT BAKER Southern Approaches

Service Road 12 (on the left) for just over 3 miles, and turn right onto Forest Service Road 13. This road ends in four miles at the "Schreibers Meadow" trailhead. (Note: The road to the trailhead is well-marked, so it might be easier to follow the signs than the above description.)

The Baker Pass Trail was recently named as one of the most abused trails in North America. It is very important that you minimize your impact in this heavily-used area.

Easton Glacier   4-6 hrs

From the Baker Pass Trail trailhead, hike 3 mi to Morovitz Meadow, where an off-trail route climbs the "Railroad Grade" moraine upward to the Easton Glacier. Camping is available on the Railroad Grade or near Morovitz Meadow. Camp on permanent snow or established bivouac sites; don't camp in Morovitz Meadow.

From the head of the Railroad Grade, ascend the glacier wherever there appears to be the fewest crevasses (the glacier is usually less-crevassed on the west side). This route is shorter and less-demanding than the Coleman-Upper Deming route, and is a popular ski ascent and descent. You may want to cross upper Deming Glacier, depending upon snow and crevasse conditions.

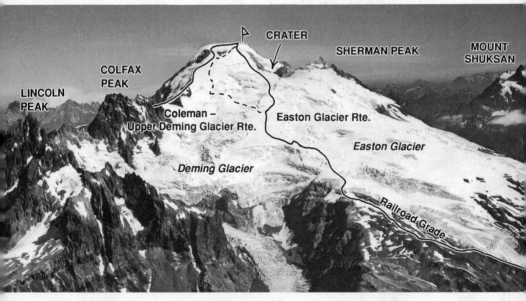

Mount Baker's Easton Glacier.   Photo: Austin Post, U.S. Geological Survey

Mount Baker 45

Boulder Ridge Trail Approach

Boulder Ridge Trail 605 is used to approach the Boulder Glacier route. To reach the trail, take the Baker Lake-Grandy Lake Road north (it becomes Forest Service Road 11 in about 12 mi). At about 16 mi from Highway 20, just past where the road crosses Boulder Creek, turn left up Forest Service Road 1130. After a mile and a half, turn sharply left onto Forest Service Road 1131. That road ends in just more than two miles at the Boulder Ridge Trailhead. Hike the trail until it ends in a small meadow, from which you access Boulder Ridge and continue cross-country to the glacier. Bivouac at one of several possible sites along the ridge.

Boulder Glacier   6-8 hrs

This route has several variations. The Boulder-Park Cleaver is crevasse-free and thus more popular. Climb the cleaver, then angle left onto the Boulder Glacier headwall,

Mount Baker's Boulder Glacier and Sherman Crater. Photo: Austin Post, U.S. Geological Survey.

above Sherman Crater, which leads to the summit. You can climb Boulder Glacier directly, but with greater exposure to avalanches, mudflows from the crater, and crevasses.

A steep and challenging finish is to climb the Park Glacier headwall from the head of the cleaver. It may be very difficult to pass the bergschrund, and the 60° snow-ice slope above the bergschrund is difficult to protect. Not for the squeamish!

Ptarmigan Ridge Trail Approach

Ptarmigan Ridge Trail 683 is commonly used to approach routes on the northeast side of Mount Baker. Take State Highway 542 from Bellingham to its end to reach the trailhead. The trail leads to Camp Kiser in 4.75 mi. From Camp Kiser, cross Sholes Glacier and upper Landes Cleaver to the Rainbow Glacier, and continue in the direction of whichever route you are climbing. Start early from Camp Kiser, or bivouac higher, as the routes from here are quite long. All approaches involve glacier travel, so rope up as necessary.

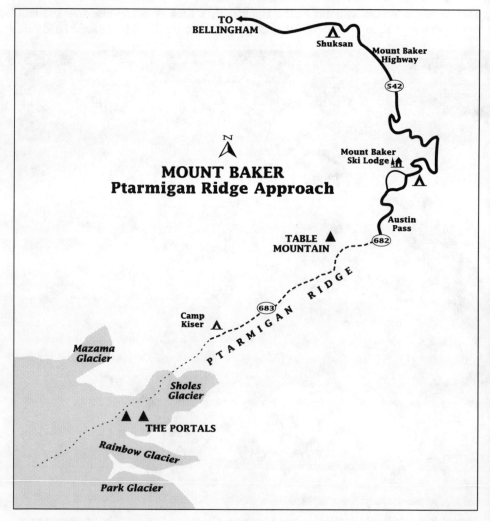

Mount Baker 47

The **Park Glacier** route (; 8 hrs) was pioneered by the legendary Joe Morovitz in 1892, solo, using a rifle butt to hack steps in the ice. Ascend the Park Glacier to a 40° snow-ice slope that is usually passed via the far right flank, close to The Cockscomb. Rockfall and avalanche hazard.

The Cockscomb (; 10-12 hrs) is a disintegrating pinnacle situated at the head of a large cleaver dividing the Park and Roosevelt Glaciers. The route does not climb directly over the rock formation, but skirts it on the east side, via steep (40°) snow (on Park Glacier's headwall). Climb an ice ridge above the Cockscomb to the summit plateau, as for Park Glacier. Rockfall hazard

The **Roosevelt Headwall** route (④; 10-12 hrs) can be approached from either Mt. Baker Trail or Camp Kiser. Continue up the upper Roosevelt Glacier. The route varies with the season, but is commonly heavily crevassed steep ice particularly at the bergschrund (which may be impassable). Grade III. Icefall hazard.

North Ridge ★ 10-12 hrs

The North Ridge route is a Mount Baker classic. All things considered, it is perhaps the finest route on Mount Baker, although some argue that Coleman Headwall is the better outing for serious climbers.

From the Mount Baker Trail, cross the Coleman Glacier laterally to the base of the ridge. The directness of your approach to the ridge will be dictated by prevailing crevasse patterns. From here, ascend snow and ice slopes closely right, on the headwall side. A few obstacles, including an ice cliff, lead to easier climbing, though the bergschrund may be difficult to pass. The ice cliff is encountered upon gaining the ridge, and may involve one-half to three-quarters of a pitch varying between 45° and 60° ice; it may sometimes be avoided, as conditions permit. The condition of the ice cliff varies, so be prepared for anything, including retreat. At the top of the ice cliff, most parties veer left to avoid summit dome crevasses. Grade III.

Coleman Glacier Headwall ★ 8-10 hrs

The Coleman Glacier headwall rises 2,000 feet, and is consistently steep, averaging over 40°. It has become a very popular climb despite its menacing nature.

Approach as for the North Ridge route to the base of the central portion of the Coleman Glacier headwall. The route climbs either of two standard variations reported in *Cascade Alpine Guide,* but several other variations have been done, all of which pass through steep ice, rock bands, crevasses and ice cliffs. All involve similar climbing over continuously steep snow, ice and rock bands, with similar risks of avalanches and falling rock and ice. The headwall should be well-frozen during your attempt. Grade IV.

This face is committing and challenging. Passing the upper ice cliffs can be troublesome. Crevasse conditions approaching the headwall often are a determining factor in a successful ascent. A bergschrund sometimes prevents access to the face. When the bergschrund is impassable, some parties have crossed over the lower portion of Roman Nose to access the headwall.

Other Coleman Glacier Headwall Routes

The **Roman Nose** (④; 8-10 hrs) is a rotten cleaver situated on the southwest (right) margin of the headwall. Stay high to reach a gully on the right side that accesses the cleaver crest. Most have found easier passage just left of the crest, via steep (40°-60°) snow-ice slopes. Passing rotten rock bands is the crux, no matter how you do it (unprotected Class 5.6 reported). Like other volcanic cleavers, it is best to climb this route during extended cold weather, with ample snow or ice holding loose rock in place. Grade III. Rockfall hazard.

The **Roman Moustache** (③; 6-8 hrs; rockfall, icefall) is a more recent variation of the Coleman Glacier route. From the Coleman-Deming Saddle (or just below), climb to the slight gully between the pumice ridge and the **Roman Nose,** continuing directly to the summit dome. It is a short, steep climb (averages 45°) with some icefall or rockfall danger. Usually, the only obstacle is a late-season crevasse halfway up, which is commonly passed on the left. Grade II.

Mount Baker

The Coleman Glacier Headwall of Mount Baker. Photo: Austin Post, U.S. Geological Survey.

50   Glacier Peak

Secluded Glacier Peak, another Washington giant.   Photo: Austin Post, U. S. Geological Survey

Chapter Three:
Glacier Peak
Washington, 10,541 ft./3213m

Tucked away within the interior of the Cascade Range of central Washington, Glacier Peak is the most remote of the peaks in this book. Indeed, no road penetrates within eight miles of the mountain; many approach hikes are more than 10 miles long, and from Puget Sound the peak barely stands out from lesser surrounding mountains. If you didn't know better, you would not guess it was one of Washington's high volcanoes. Nevertheless, Glacier Peak, at 10,541 ft., is one of the Cascade giants, and is highly visible from nearly all points along the Washington Cascade crest. Local Indians knew the mountain as "Dakobed" (one translation says "Great Parent") and "Takomed" or "Takobud," a generic term meaning "White Mountain."

Like Garibaldi, Glacier Peak is a heavily-glaciated, significantly-eroded dacite volcano. The mountain has a long history of building and explosive eruptions, the last major eruption occurring at least 12,000 years ago. That eruption, though not as violent as the 1980 eruption of Mount St. Helens, did manage to deposit volcanic ash as far away as Alberta, and spewed debris over a wide area to the southeast. There is no evidence of significant eruptions since that time – except for the extrusion of Disappointment Peak, a dacite plug – but hot springs near the base of the peak are a sign that volcanic forces are still at work beneath the mountain (although the springs have been cooling significantly). At least one geologist considers Glacier Peak the least likely of the Washington volcanoes to erupt in the near future; others are not so certain.

The volume of glacial ice and the composition of Glacier Peak have resulted in very heavy erosion. The summit crater has been worn away to a gentle saddle ("Crater Gap") between the Scimitar Glacier on the west and the Chocolate Glacier on the east. Sections of the crater rim still exist in the summit formation and several craggy points to the north. There is evidence to suggest the mountain was once a bit higher than its present altitude; however, it is thought that the eruption 12,000 years ago, or earlier eruptions, and not glaciation alone, lowered the elevation of Glacier Peak.

Glacier Peak was first climbed in 1898, long after the first ascents of every other non-technical Cascade volcano, when U.S. Geological Survey surveyor Thomas Gerdine, along with four others, made an ascent to place a survey marker at the summit. Professor I.C. Russel climbed Glacier Peak later that year. In 1906, A.L. Cool and C.E. Rusk climbed what is now known as the Cool Glacier. A Mountaineers' reconnaissance team ascended the Cool-Chocolate Cleaver in 1910. Many of the early ascents were made from the south or southeast, mostly via the Disappointment Peak route.

Because of its remoteness and its unassuming skyline presence, Glacier Peak is not as popular an ascent as most other Cascade volcanoes. However, it is enjoyable, and mostly

Glacier Peak

> Information on the Glacier Peak Wilderness may be obtained from:
>
> Darrington Ranger District (206) 436-1155
> 1405 Emmens Street
> Darrington, WA 98241
>
> Supervisor's Office (206) 442-0170
> Mt. Baker-Snoqualmie National Forest
> 915 Second Avenue, Room 442
> Seattle, WA 98174

private, except for popular weekend routes. Glacier Peak is regarded as an easy climb by most, but it has had its share of accidents and fatalities due to falls, crevasses and poor weather, and should not be taken lightly, especially considering its remoteness. Local rescuers are reluctant to fly helicopters high on Glacier Peak. Climbers must be self-sufficient on Glacier Peak, perhaps more so than on some of the other Cascade volcanoes, where rescues typically are more forthcoming.

The mountain is the centerpiece of the Glacier Peak Wilderness, which was established in 1964 with the passage of the Wilderness Act. Permits are no longer required for overnight visits.

For more information on routes not thoroughly described in this guide, please refer to Fred Beckey's *Cascade Alpine Guide Vol. 2* (The Mountaineers, 1989).

Climbers ascend the Sitkum Glacier. Photo: Jeff Smoot

Glacier Peak 53

Rating details appear on pages 4 through 7 of the Introduction.

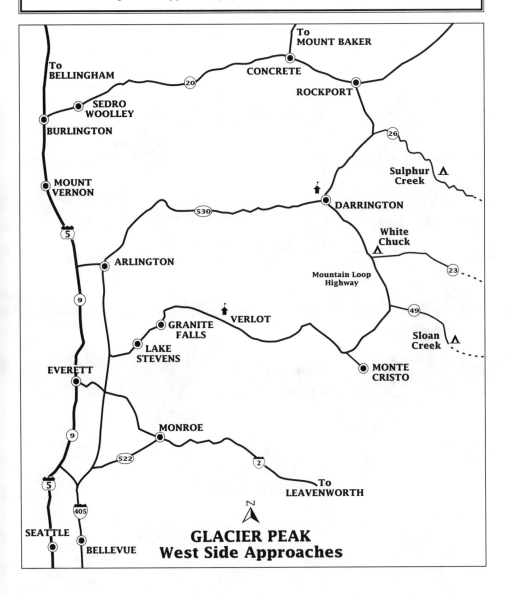

**GLACIER PEAK
West Side Approaches**

Glacier Peak

White Chuck Trail Approach

The customary approach for westside routes on Glacier Peak is via White Chuck Trail 643 to Kennedy Hot Springs. Drive State Highway 530 east from I-5 to Darrington. Follow the Mountain Loop Highway south from Darrington about 9 mi to a bridge crossing the Sauk River. Once across the river, take White Chuck Road 23 east 10.5 mi to the White Chuck Trailhead. Hike the trail 5 mi to Kennedy Hot Springs junction.

To approach Sitkum Glacier and Disappointment Peak routes from the Kennedy Hot Springs junction, follow Upper White Chuck Trail 643A, which forks to the left and switchbacks steeply up the wooded ridge from the hot springs trail junction. After about 2 mi, Trail 643A meets the Pacific Crest Trail (PCT). Go left .5 mile to the climbers' trail to Sitkum Glacier; go right about 5 mi to White Chuck Glacier.

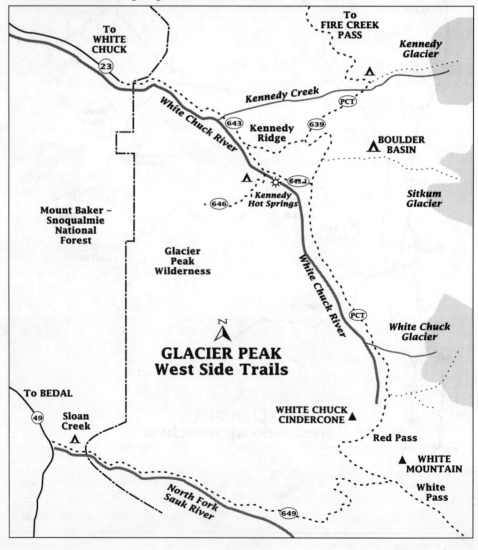

Sitkum Glacier ① 4-6 hrs

Sitkum Glacier is the most popular route on Glacier Peak because of its direct approach hike. A steep climbers' trail from the PCT reaches "Boulder Basin," the customary camping area in a small basin near the toe of the northern lobe of Sitkum Glacier. Protect your food from hungry marmots, who have taken a liking to climbers' chow. Some parties prefer to camp higher up, at the toe of the glacier. Some make a round trip from basecamp at Kennedy Hot Springs, but this is very long. (One climber did a one-day round trip ascent of this route from Seattle, but this is an exception.)

Because Boulder Basin is a heavily-used base camp, it suffers from some adverse impacts, most notably improperly disposed human waste. There is a pit toilet here, but prior to July, it is buried in snow. Parties bivouacking here in early season should be mindful of this problem and take measures to minimize it.

From the basin, several routes are possible. Most continue directly up to the terminus of the glacier. The customary route stays on the left flank of the lower lobe of Sitkum Glacier (the right flank is more-heavily crevassed), avoiding mid-height crevasses, then traverses the upper lobe to a saddle above Sitkum Spire (which reportedly has been climbed, despite its rotten appearance). From the saddle, the route continues up snow or

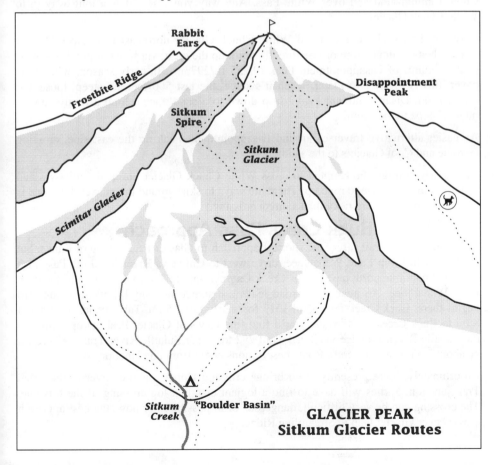

GLACIER PEAK
Sitkum Glacier Routes

pumice on the ridge, or just left on Scimitar Glacier. Many parties continue directly from the glacier to the summit rather than crossing the saddle.

Other variations from Boulder Basin, which climb ice and snow gullies farther right, are not often done because they have higher rockfall hazard and take two or three hours longer than the main route.

A soak in sometimes-crowded Kennedy Hot Springs is popular on the hike out, more so if poor weather prevents an ascent. The springs are not as unsanitary as some reports warn, but at only 94°F, they are disappointingly tepid.

South Ridge/Disappointment Peak 8-10 hrs

This was the first-ascent route of Glacier Peak, and is used by modern parties only because it does not require significant glacier travel. It is a very long route, not popular, and not necessarily easy.

The shortest approach is via White Chuck Trail, as for Sitkum Glacier. From the Upper White Chuck/PCT junction, hike south about 5 mi to where a broad basin gives immediate access to White Chuck Glacier. A longer alternative hikes in from Sloan Creek Campground and over White Pass. Any way you come, it is a long way in to White Chuck Glacier.

Traverse the usually-uncrevassed White Chuck Glacier northeast to a gap ("Glacier Gap"), then continue more or less directly north up the crest, via snow or pumice slopes, to the summit of Disappointment Peak (9,755 ft./2973m). In early season, with snow cover, this is pretty easy; later, when it's scree, the last 500 feet are steep, loose and scary. From Disappointment Peak, drop down to a saddle and climb a final snow or pumice slope to the summit.

An easier alternative traverses around Disappointment Peak on the east side, crossing Gerdine and Cool Glaciers to the saddle.

Although you might be tempted to cross White Chuck Glacier unroped, crevasses and sinkholes make it wise to rope up. There are ways to skirt around the glacier, but none is easy and some are more risky than a direct crossing.

Buck Creek Pass Approach

Buck Creek Pass Trail offers the shortest approach to Glacier Peak's eastern flanks, but not by much. From Lake Wenatchee, drive west to Chiwawa River Road 62. Pass Fish Lake and continue north past Phelps Creek Campground to Trinity, about 24 miles from Lake Wenatchee. An abandoned road leads a distance beyond Trinity, and the trail begins there. Buck Creek Pass Trail 1513 forks off after 1.5 mi. Take the left fork about 8 mi to Buck Creek Pass, where you'll find fine views of Glacier Peak. Drop 3 mi into the Suiattle River drainage via Triad Trail 792 to Upper Suiattle River Trail 798 (you'll be about 3.5 mi from its end). Route descriptions begin from this junction.

Unfortunately, there presently is no bridge crossing Upper Suiattle River at the Triad Trail junction. Parties will have to find a logjam or fallen log crossing, if there is one. The crossing can be very difficult, dangerous or impossible. For now, the best approach crosses over Glacier Gap to Streamline Ridge.

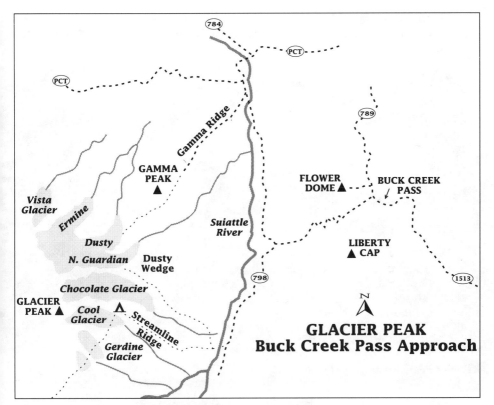

East Side Summit Routes

The **Chocolate – Cool Cleaver** route (②; 4-6 hrs) climbs the cleaver dividing Chocolate and Cool glaciers. Any way you come, expect to hike all day on your approach. From the Triad Trail junction, hike south until just across Chocolate Creek. A hard-to-find trail leads up Chocolate Creek Basin; bushwhacking through the basin provides access to Streamline Ridge, the gentle ridge between the termini of the Cool and Chocolate Glaciers. Traverse the Cool Glacier above South Guardian Rock to the cleaver, and scend directly to the summit. In late season, without snow cover, the route is not recommended. If you use this as a descent route, be careful to leave the cleaver well above South Guardian Rock.

The **Cool Glacier** route (①; 4-6 hrs) climbs the glacier that descends southeast from the Disappointment Peak saddle. It is named for A.L. Cool, who first ascened it in 1906 with Claude E. Rusk (Rusk originally named this the Chocolate Glacier). The route climbs Cool Glacier toward the Disappointment Peak saddle, then snow or pumice slopes to the summit.

The **Chocolate Glacier** route (②; 6-8 hrs) follows the broad, crevassed glacier that descends east from the crater gap. Traverse the glacier northward beneath South Guardian Rock toward North Guardian Rock, then cut back and up the broad part of the glacier to the crater gap. Crevasses are abundant, but corridors may allow reasonable passage until late season.

The **North Guardian Glacier** route (②; 6-8 hrs) involves traversing the North Guardian, Dusty and upper Ermine Glaciers to Frostbite Ridge via a few possible variations.

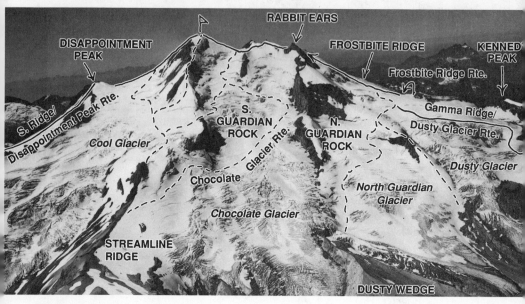

Glacier Peak's remote east side. Photo: Austin Post, U.S. Geological Survey.

Suiattle River Approach

Glacier Peak's northern routes may be approached via Upper Suiattle River. Take Forest Service Road 26, which leaves State Highway 530 about 6 mi north of Darrington, just north of where the highway crosses the Sauk River. The road follows the Suiattle River about 25 mi to Sulphur Creek Campground. Suiattle River Trailhead is another mile down the road.

Hike Suiattle River Trail 784 about 9 mi to a junction with Image Lake/Miner's Ridge Trail 785. Route descriptions begin from this junction. You can approach eastside routes (Cool, Chocolate Glaciers) by continuing on Upper Suiattle River Trail 798 7 mi to to the Chocolate Creek junction (rather than approaching from Buck Creek Pass); this approach saves driving time if coming from Puget Sound, but is a longer hike.

Suiattle River Road 26 washed out recently, and the Forest Service is debating whether to repair the road. If not repaired, add about 11 mi of hiking from the washout to the trailhead, which would certainly render this an unlikely approach for most climbers.

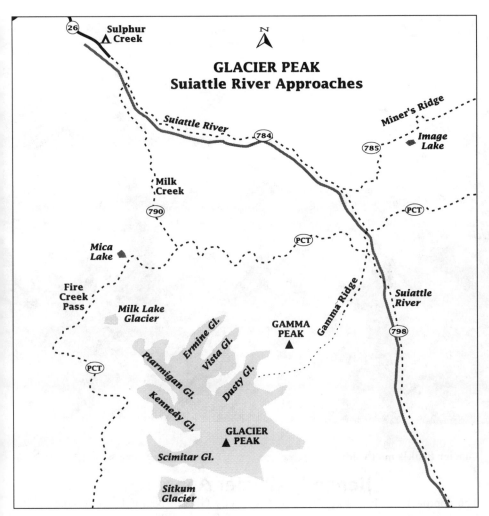

Gamma Ridge – Dusty Glacier ★ ② 8-10 hrs

The Dusty Glacier descends to the northeast from Frostbite Ridge, and is split at its terminus by Recession Rock. Many routes are possible, depending upon crevasse conditions; all reach Frostbite Ridge eventually. This fine route is not as popular as it deserves to be.

Approach via Suiattle River Trail and the PCT to Gamma Ridge Trail 791. Hike to the trail's end, and continue cross-country up Gamma Ridge to the glacier, which you'll encounter well above its terminus. Traverse the glacier as crevasses permit to Frostbite Ridge, which is followed to the summit.

Another route, known as **Milk Creek (or Vista Glacier)** (②; 8-10 hrs), is reported in the *Cascade Alpine Guide*. It is merely another way to Frostbite Ridge, approaching from the east side by linking Ptarmigan, Vista and Ermine Glaciers via obvious gaps, and it is not often climbed. Vista Glacier is more direct and more often climbed than Milk Creek.

Glacier Peak

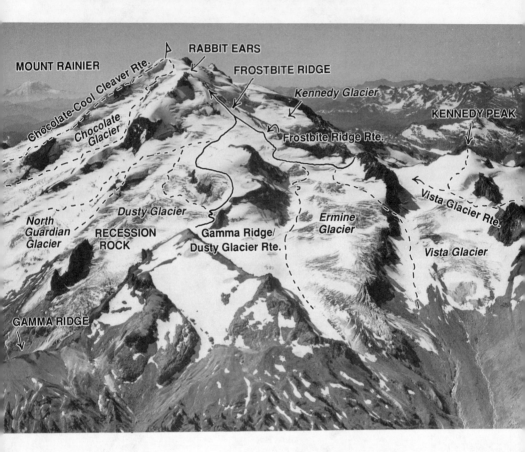

Glacier Peak's north side.
Photo: Austin Post, U. S. Geological Survey

Kennedy Glacier Approach

The approach for Frostbite Ridge and Kennedy Glacier begins by following White Chuck Trail from Kennedy Hot Springs. After following White Chuck Trail for about 5 mi, take Kennedy Ridge Trail 639 (see map on page 54) 2 mi to the PCT. Continue 2 mi northeast to upper Kennedy Ridge; a climbers' trail leads from here to Kennedy Glacier. There are campsites at the trail junction, and many others along the upper ridge and near the glacier terminus.

Frostbite Ridge ★ ② 6-8 hrs

While this route is named "Frostbite Ridge," it's only different from many of the preceding routes in how you approach the ridge. Frostbite Ridge is an interesting climb that is deservingly popular.

The route has several variations. You can climb Kennedy Glacier partway and traverse to the Ptarmigan Glacier gap; stay high on Kennedy Ridge, skirting around Kennedy Peak on the north side via Ptarmigan Glacier (as for "Milk Creek Route"); or gain Frostbite Ridge directly from Kennedy Glacier via an obvious saddle (the shortest, most popular variation). Another possibility follows the PCT north toward Fire Creek Pass to the Ptarmigan Glacier, then continues as for the "Milk Creek Route."

Once you reach Frostbite Ridge proper, continue up the ridge crest (or just east of the ridge), which attains its maximum angle about 20 feet below the Rabbit Ears. Pass through the Rabbit Ears and downclimb Class 3 rock to a notch. A short vertical snow step usually must be passed here. Continue across the crater rim to the summit.

Kennedy Glacier ★ ② 6-8 hrs

Another of Glacier Peak's popular routes, Kennedy Glacier is more rugged than Sitkum Glacier but equally accessible and said by some to be more enjoyable. Approach as for Frostbite Ridge, then climb the Kennedy Glacier. The route is moderately crevassed, but is usually very straightforward.

A variation recorded in the *Cascade Alpine Guide* climbs the south arm of the Kennedy Glacier directly to the summit ridge; it is still not known whether this variation has been climbed, although because Beckey included it in his guide, it very probably has by now. The Kennedy Cleaver is reported as a route, although it appears to be one of the worst possible routes up the mountain.

The **Scimitar Glacier** route (③; 6 hrs) follows the narrow glacier descending west from Crater Gap. A bergschrund about midway between Sitkum Ridge and the summit is usually the only obstacle. Grade II.

Mount Rainier, with Little Tahoma Peak in the foreground.

Photo: Austin Post, U. S. Geological Survey.

Chapter Four:
Mount Rainier
Washington, 14,411 ft./4392m

Mount Rainier is arguably the King of the Cascade volcanoes. Certainly, the other peaks have their charms, but Rainier stands supreme in the hearts and minds all who view it from near or afar. It is the highest volcano in the contiguous United States. The mountain was for many years measured at 14,410 ft., but in 1988, a new satellite measurement added just over one foot to that height. Either way, Rainier is still the highest. It is visible from almost any high vantage in western Washington, and is best known by its profile from Seattle, as depicted on Rainier Beer labels. The uniqueness and grandeur of Mount Rainier and its surrounding peaks and forests was recognized early enough that the area was preserved by the establishment of a national park on March 2, 1899.

Because of its height, and due to its proximity to the Pacific Ocean (only about 100mi/175km distant), Mount Rainier truly creates its own weather. Rising high into the thinning atmosphere, Mount Rainier stands directly in the path of prevailing moisture-laden marine winds, which results in some unusual weather that seems unique to the mountain, including lenticular cloud "halos" or "caps" that sometimes settle on the summit of the mountain for several days while the remainder of the sky is clear. This proximity to wet marine air also accounts for the high volume of snowfall on Mount Rainier. Indeed, Paradise (5,400 feet), on the mountain's southern slope, has had world-record snow depths, and Paradise Inn is frequently buried up to its three-story roof (early-summer guests commonly enter the inn via a snow tunnel). The weather can be quite unpredictable. "Perfect" days often become cold, windy and cloudy with little warning. Winter and spring storms frequently deposit several feet of new wet snow on the mountain, and winds can reach very high velocity at any time of year.

Mount Rainier's glacier system, consisting of 26 major glaciers covering more than 35 square miles, is the largest single-mountain glacier system in the United States outside of Alaska (although statistically, Mount Baker is reported to have a greater mass of ice within its 12 glaciers). However, Mount Rainier's mantle of ice belies its fiery origins. Geologists speculate that the Mount Rainier volcano once rose to a height of over 16,000 feet. A subsequent violent eruption, possibly similar to that of neighboring Mount St. Helens in 1980, or a caldera collapse as occurred with Mounts Mazama and Tehama, reduced this earlier summit cone, leaving a wide crater that later erupted to form the present cone and two well-preserved craters that now make up the summit of Mount Rainier.

Mount Rainier has been predominately dormant during recorded history, but it is by no means extinct. The fumaroles that warmed Stevens and Van Trump on their first ascent

Mount Rainier

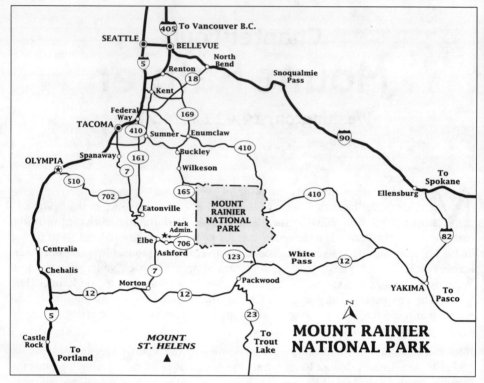

of the peak still spew steam from the summit-crater firn caves. Heat fluctuations within the mountain sometimes cause the melting of glacial ice and the heating of mud-like volcanic rock, producing devastating mud flows. Indeed, mudflows have been singled out by geologists as the greatest volcanic threat to nearby lowland populations. The Osceola Mudflow of about 6,000 years ago buried what are present-day Enumclaw and Puyallup under a thick layer of volcanic concrete. More recently, the Nisqually, Kautz and South Tahoma Glaciers have discharged mudflows and outburst floods.

More than 4,000 people climb Mount Rainier each year, and almost twice that number attempt the mountain. About 30% of these climbers are guided by Rainier Mountaineering, Inc., the park's sole guide service. Most ascents take the "dog routes" of Disappointment Cleaver and Emmons Glacier (most guided ascents are via Disappointment Cleaver). Often, after a spell of good weather, climbers can follow deep trail-like snow trenches left by dozens of preceding parties all the way to the summit. Those seeking a bit more adventure should avoid Camp Muir and the above two routes. Though these routes have dangers and challenges, they are as different to most other routes on Rainier as modern freeways are to country roads.

For further information about climbing Mount Rainier, contact:

Mount Rainier National Park (206) 569-2211
Tahoma Woods, Star Route
Ashford, WA 98304

Mount Rainier

Rating details appear on pages 4 through 7 of the Introduction.

Because of its prominence and attractiveness to lowlanders, Mount Rainier has been the site of many climbing accidents and fatalities. It is not more dangerous than the other peaks, but the sheer number of climbers who visit Mount Rainier greatly increase the statistical chances of accidents occuring. Each year, it seems, at least a few people are killed on Mount Rainier. For those wishing to learn the details of these accidents, an in-depth accounting of all known fatalities on Mount Rainier is contained in Dee Molenaar's *The Challenge of Rainier*. Read this before you attempt to climb Mount Rainier; you might learn something which could save you from repeating someone else's mistakes.

Many deaths on Mount Rainier can be attributed solely to inexperience and folly. The mountain is no place for unguided inexperienced climbers. Also, conditioning can play a major role in climbing safety. Climbers should be in good physical shape before attempting the climb, as fatigue and sickness can lead to injury or death at high elevations.

Climbers going higher than 10,000 feet, traveling off trail, or camping on glaciers are required to register and obtain permits in advance, and to check out upon their return. The park service limits the number of people occupying popular campsites, such as Camp Muir and Camp Schurman, and permits are issued on a first-come, first-served basis (no reservations accepted). Party size is limited to 12 persons. Climbers under the age of 18 years must have written parental consent. Parties of two or more are required above high camps. Solo climbers must obtain advance written permission from the park superintendent. Guiding for a fee is prohibited, except for the RMI concession. Any violation of these regulations is punishable by a fine.

The author gratefully acknowledges the assistance of Dee Molenaar, author of *The Challenge of Rainier*, and of the National Park Service, in preparing this chapter. For more information on routes not thoroughly described in this guide, please see Fred Beckey's *Cascade Alpine Guide Vol. 1* (The Mountaineers, 1987).

Camp Muir Approach

Most routes on Mount Rainier's east side are approached via Camp Muir from Paradise, including Nisqually Icefall and Ice Cliff, Gibraltar Ledge and the Disappointment Cleaver route. Camp Muir was named for John Muir, who, recognizing the presence of light pumice on the ground as an indication of shelter from wind, selected the site during his 1888 ascent of the mountain. Camp Muir typically is overcrowded. The park service permits only 100 people per night at Camp Muir, and reservations are not accepted. It has a public shelter available on a first-come, first-in basis, plus rock windbreaks for tents. Toilet facilities are in place here – use them!

The ascent to Camp Muir begins on Panorama Point Trail, which is paved part of the way. From the Panorama Point Junction, follow Pebble Creek to trail's end, where a climbers' trail continues to the Muir Snowfield. Ascend the snowfield toward Moon Rocks, then to the saddle occupied by Camp Muir. Crevasses sometimes lurk here, particularly close to Nisqually Glacier, so beware! The route usually is easy to follow, particularly on sunny weekends, but during poor weather it is easy to become lost.

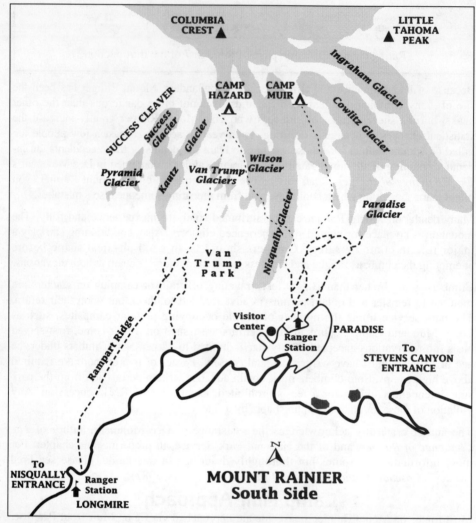

Taking compass bearings during the ascent may avoid routefinding troubles on the way down.

Disappointment Cleaver 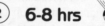 6-8 hrs

Disappointment Cleaver presently is the most frequently traveled route on Mount Rainier. More than half of all annual ascents of Mount Rainier take this route, as it is usually the route used by RMI for guided ascents. Non-guided climbers are urged to stay off this route on summer weekends to avoid traffic jams.

The route (also known as the "guide route," "RMI route," "dog route" and "D.C.") traverses the Cowlitz Glacier laterally to Cathedral Gap, then continues across the Ingraham Glacier to Disappointment Cleaver, which is climbed (on snow in early season, on loose rock later) or skirted on the right (as crevasses permit). From the cleaver's head, continue via Ingraham Glacier to the east crater rim (the "summit" for some parties), then across to Columbia Crest.

This route has icefall hazard below Disappointment Cleaver, and some rockfall danger on the cleaver. Avalanche danger often is high in early season. Variations include going through Cadaver Gap, which has higher rockfall danger; and a direct route up Ingraham Glacier from Cathedral Gap, which has high icefall danger.

Gibraltar Ledge (③; 6-8 hrs) was the route most used in early ascents of Mount Rainier, and was very popular until 1936, when a large portion of the ledge fell away. Wrote the late Joseph Hazard of Gibraltar Ledge in 1911, *"This route is not recommended. At its best it presents danger that cannot be avoided by foresight or skill."* The route traverses a wide ledge to a forced rappel or downclimb, where a lower shelf traverses to gullies that regain the upper portion of the ledge. Regaining the ledge during the descent is usually accomplished with a fixed rope. Grade II, Class 4. Rockfall hazard.

Mount Rainier's south face.   Photo: Austin Post, U.S. Geological Survey

Camp Schurman Approach

Camp Schurman (9,500 feet) is at the head of Steamboat Prow, where it cleaves the Emmons and Winthrop Glaciers. The Emmons Glacier and Russell Cliff routes begin from here. The park service presently permits only 35 climbers per night at Camp Schurman (including Emmons Flats). Reservations are not accepted. Camp Schurman has a climbers' hut (for emergency use only) equipped with a radio; the camp also has toilets (use them!), and a number of rock windbreaks and other existing campsites. High winds have stolen more than one tent here. Many climbers prefer to camp about 300-500 feet above Camp Schurman on the glacier ("Emmons Flats"), to get an earlier start and avoid the crowds below. Sanitation is a big problem here.

Approach Camp Schurman via White River Campground and the Glacier Basin Trail. From trail's end, continue up a climbers' path to the terminus of the Inter Glacier. Ascend the glacier (rope up, there are crevasses) obliquely left to the gap between Mount Ruth and Steamboat Prow, the site of the formerly-popular Camp Curtis. From here, either descend to the Emmons Glacier and along Steamboat Prow to Camp Schurman, or continue to a point just left of the summit of Steamboat Prow, and descend the most feasible-looking gullies to Camp Schurman.

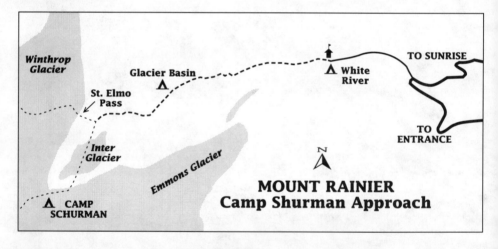

Emmons – Winthrop Glacier   5-7 hrs

This route possibly was ascended in 1855, definitely in 1884. This long glacier trudge presently is the second most-popular route on Mount Rainier.

From Camp Schurman, ascend left on the Emmons Glacier to "The Corridor," a usually unbroken pathway between crevasses that ends about halfway to the summit. Continue up the glacier as crevasses permit. The final obstacle, the bergschrund, usually may be passed on either end.

There are few appreciable dangers on this route, other than those normally encountered on long glacier climbs (e.g., crevasses, random icefall, avalanches).

The **Russell Cliff** route (④; 10-12 hrs) also can be reached from Camp Schurman. In September 1989, Russell Cliff suffered a massive rockfall that scattered an estimated 2.6 million cubic yards of debris across the lower half of the Winthrop Glacier. However, the rockfall does not appear to have affected the Russell Cliff routes. One variation crosses a steep snow-ice slope directly above Russell Cliff to upper Curtis Ridge via a wide gully. The other climbs directly through the higher headwall, passing rock bands. Grade III, with rockfall and avalanche danger.

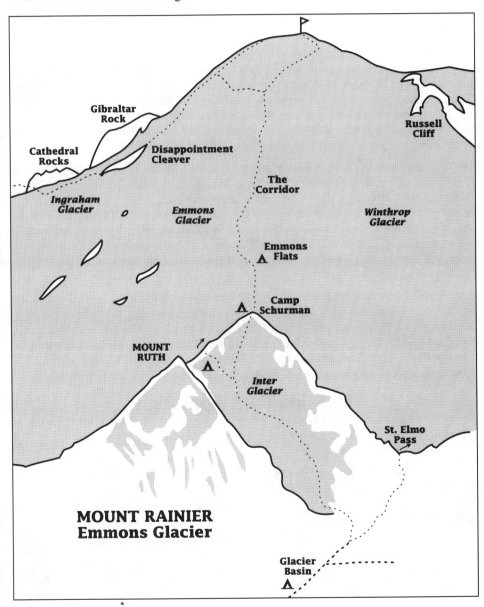

**MOUNT RAINIER
Emmons Glacier**

St. Elmo Pass Approach

St. Elmo Pass is the saddle dividing The Wedge from Burroughs Mountain, and is used to reach the Curtis Ridge and upper Carbon Glacier routes, including Willis Wall and Liberty Ridge. Approach via White River Campground and the Glacier Basin Trail. From trail's end, scramble over St. Elmo Pass and cross the Winthrop Glacier. In late season, this may not be feasible due to rockfall debris on the glacier. In early season, snowcover prevents problems of this sort. (See map on page 68.)

None of the routes described below is recommended because of extreme rockfall, avalanche and icefall danger.

The condition of the **Curtis Ridge** route (⑤; 12+ hrs; rockfall) is not known due to the recent rockfall, but it appears intact. Curtis Ridge has been moderately popular as one of the most technical routes on Mount Rainier, despite its reputation as a "suicide ridge." The route has several reported variations, involving possible direct aid, water ice, loose Class 5 climbing and direct stonefall. Above the first rock bands, the route follows snow and ice slopes and gullies, weaving through or over the rock bands. The final rock band has a steep gully, allowing passage to the upper ridge. Grade V, Class 5 or aid.

Of the north faces in North America, Mount Rainier's **Willis Wall** is one of the most infamous, and is assuredly the most appalling. Rising nearly 4,000 feet above the Carbon Glacier, Willis Wall is a dark, foreboding depression of loose rock that is regularly scoured by immense ice avalanches from the 300-foot-high ice cliffs hanging over the wall. Despite the objective hazards, the Willis Wall is a popular objective, in theory if not in practice. To climb Willis Wall and survive seems to automatically elevate one to "immortal" status among northwest climbers. If you must climb these routes, please refer to *Cascade Alpine Guide Vol. 1*.

Because of the difficult technical nature and extreme objective danger of all routes on Willis Wall, you should bring ice screws, pitons, helmets, bivouac gear and lots of luck. Most routes on Willis Wall are Grade V with poorly-protected Class 5 rock. The routes are: **East Route** (⑤; 12+ hrs; rockfall, icefall); **East Rib** (⑤; 12+ hrs; rockfall, icefall); **Central Rib** (⑤; 12+ hrs; rockfall, icefall); **West Rib** (⑤; 12+ hrs; rockfall, icefall); and **Thermogenesis** (③; 8+ hrs; rockfall, icefall).

Moraine Park Approach

Some parties approach Willis Wall and Liberty Ridge via Moraine Park, although this is a bit longer than crossing St. Elmo Pass, which is more popular.

To approach via Moraine Park, begin from Ipsut Creek Campground and hike the Wonderland Trail into Moraine Park. Continue hiking cross-country from just below the saddle where the trail drops to Mystic Lake. Go through Moraine Park, to a bivouac site above the upper Carbon Glacier at about 8,000 feet (there are some stone windbreaks here – don't build any more!). The glacier is easily accessible from here.

Mount Rainier 71

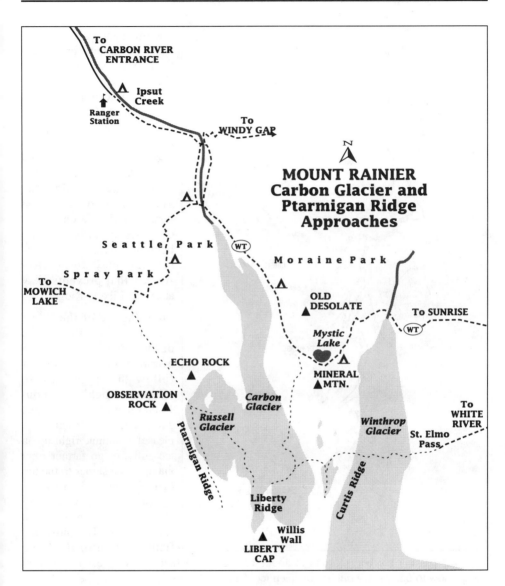

Liberty Ridge ★ ③ 12+ hrs

Liberty Ridge easily is the most popular north face route on Mount Rainier. It is included in *Fifty Classic Climbs of North America,* which has no doubt added to its overwhelming popularity. First ascended by Jim Borrow, Arnie Campbell and Ome Daiber in 1935, it was not repeated for 20 years.

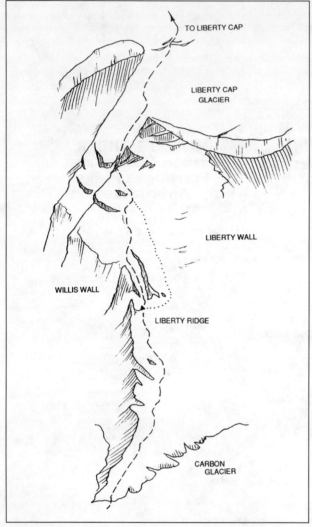

The usual approach is via St. Elmo Pass, then across Curtis Ridge and the Carbon Glacier to the toe of Liberty Ridge. Alternatively, approach via Moraine Park, then cross the glacier to the toe of the ridge, as crevasses permit. Watch for potential ice avalanches from Willis Wall while crossing the glacier. The route is best done in early season, before crevasses on Carbon Glacier become difficult. A bergschrund may form after August that prevents easy access to Liberty Ridge.

From the toe of the ridge, ascend snow-ice slopes right of the ridge crest, crossing over rock steps in places, or follow the ridge crest to "Thumb Rock" at about 11,000 feet (this is the usual campsite; keep it sanitary, please). Continue right up an ice gully, or go farther right via open ice slopes to the top of the final rocks ("Black Pyramid") and the Liberty Cap Glacier. Continue to Liberty Cap. The most difficult portion of the route involves passing the bergschrund at about 13,000 feet, which can vary each year from steep snow to one or two pitches of steep ice. Grade IV.

This route is longer and more serious than many parties anticipate. Perhaps due to its "classic" status, it has lured many an unsuspecting climber to his demise. This route has rockfall danger, and serious avalanche conditions after fresh snowfall. Some parties descend Liberty Ridge, while others prefer the Winthrop-Emmons Glacier route.

The **Liberty Wall** route (5; 12+ hrs) climbs the headwall immediately right of Liberty Ridge, and passes through the Liberty Cap Glacier ice cliff. Two variations have been reported. Risky, with rockfall and icefall danger. Grade IV.

Mount Rainier

Spray Park Approach

Hike into Spray Park from Mowich Lake. Leave the trail at its high point and hike cross country to the gap between Echo Rock and Observation Rock to the Russell Glacier. Those climbing Ptarmigan Ridge should continue on Russell Glacier (just below the crest of Ptarmigan Ridge) to a bivouac site at the notch just beyond the high point. Others should drop down Russell Glacier to Carbon Glacier and the base of Liberty Wall. Russell Glacier is crevassed, so rope up!

Parties climbing Ptarmigan Ridge almost always use the Spray Park approach; parties climbing Liberty Wall have approached this way also. A shorter but more complicated approach involves cross-country hiking via Knapsack Pass to Spray Park. For Liberty Ridge, the St. Elmo Pass approach is more popular.

Spray Park suffers from overuse, so try to minimize your impact while passing through. Hike on snow whenever possible. Don't leave the trail if you don't have to.

Ptarmigan Ridge ★   10-12 hrs

This is a fine route, considering its alpine nature, continuity of line, commitment and difficulty. It was first ascended by Wolf Bauer and Jack Hossack in 1935.

The original ascent climbed ice slopes and ledges more or less directly above the bivouac site. The second party found an easier way. From camp, drop onto the North Mowich Glacier and traverse beneath the rock buttress to a prominent snow-ice corridor leading left between the rock bands (rockfall hazard). Ascend continuous snow and ice slopes, then go left through a final rock band to the Liberty Cap Glacier. Grade III.

A variation traverses under the Liberty Cap Glacier ice cliff. While more direct, this variation is much more dangerous. The most recent variation climbed the imposing ice cliff directly via a fracture on the right side. When the cliff is "in shape," two or three pitches of steep (70°) ice are the norm. Definitely not for the squeamish.

This route is quite committing and difficult. It should not be attempted except during periods when loose rock is likely held in place by snow and ice. The ice cliff variations have the additional hazard of icefall. Descents are usually made via another route (Emmons Glacier, Tahoma Glacier, Furher Finger, Disappointment Cleaver), depending on where you left your car.

Mowich Face Routes

Mowich Face is the steep wall below Liberty Cap on the west, between Ptarmigan and Sunset Ridges. The wall is consistently steep (about 40° to 50°), and like Willis Wall, has hanging ice cliffs and a propensity for stonefall. The face is commonly approached via Klapatche and St. Andrews Parks; a climbers' trail leads up Puyallup Cleaver to a traverse of the Puyallup and South Mowich Glaciers and onto the Edmunds or North Mowich Glaciers.

All routes on the Mowich Face should be attempted only during periods of snow and rock stability (the weeks between mid-June and mid-July have been suggested as best). Hanging ice and loose rock contribute to this face's difficulty and danger. Bring ice screws and helmets for all routes on Mowich Face, and pitons etc. for those with rock pitches.

Mount Rainier

From left to right, the routes are: **North Mowich Glacier Icefall** (④; 12 hrs); **North Mowich Glacier Headwall** (④; 12 hrs); **Mowich Face – Central** (④; 10 hrs); **Edmunds Glacier Headwall** (③; 8 hrs). All of these routes feature rockfall, avalanche and icefall hazard.

The prominent Sunset Ridge (③; 10-12 hrs) flanks the Mowich Face on the right. Traverse the South Mowich Flacier from the head fo Colonnade Ridge to the cleaver separating the South Mowich and Edmunds glaciers. Ascend left tof the ridge crest ia prominent snow and ice slops to the ridge crest proper. C ontinue on a rotten traverse along the crest or on snow and ice below the rest to the upper slopes. Grade III. Rockfall hazard.

Mowich Face and Ptarmigan Ridge. Photo: Austin Post, U. S. Geological Survey

The **Sunset Amphitheater** route (④; 10 hrs) ascends the large cirque at the head of the South Mowich Glacier. Its headwall is a colorful cliff of bands of andesite, pumice and ash that appear impregnable from a distance, but somewhat more feasible from Sunset Ridge. Approach via Puyallup Cleaver and continue over or around St. Andrews Rocks (rockfall hazard) to the headwall. Ascends via the shortest possible line to the icecap. Ice climbing past the ice cliff may be necessary (Grade II). Rockfall and icefall hazard.

Puyallup Cleaver Approach

All routes on the west side of Mount Rainier, north of and including the Tahoma Glacier route, are usually approached via Puyallup Cleaver. If the Westside Road is accessible, drive north from the Nisqually entrance, over Round Pass, and down to St. Andrews Creek. The shortest approach hikes Klapatche Park Trail to the Wonderland Trail, then heads south to St. Andrews Lake, where a climbers' trail leads up Puyallup Cleaver past Tokaloo Spire and Tokaloo Rock. If Westside Road is still closed due to flood damage expect very long approach hikes to west side routes. Hike the road to South Puyallup River, then go 1.5 mi to the Wonderland Trail, and 3.5 mi north to St. Andrews Lake and the climbers' trail. Continue up the cleaver, avoiding an impassable rock buttress on the left via the Puyallup Glacier. Regain the cleaver at a saddle near 9,000 feet, which is a customary bivouac site with a few stone wind shelters.

Puyallup Cleaver has suffered from overuse by climbing and cross-country hiking parties. Smaller parties are recommended to lessen impact here. Use established campsites or camp on snow to avoid further damage. "Off-site" camping will soon be citable offense!

West Side Summit Routes

The popular **Tahoma Glacier** route ★ (③; 8-10 hrs) climbs the glacier that flows through the narrow gap between Sunset Amphitheater and Tahoma Cleaver. It is not technically demanding and is most direct. From the bivouac, continue up the Puyallup Glacier left of the cleaver's crest to where the cleaver fades and the slope drops off steeply toward the Tahoma Glacier. Traverse to the central portion of the narrowing glacier and ascend more or less directly to the summit plateau.

The **Tahoma Cleaver** route (⑤; 12+ hrs) follows the prominent cleaver separating the Tahoma and South Tahoma Glaciers. Long, difficult and deservedly unpopular. Grade V, Class 4 or 5. Rockfall hazard.

Success Divide Approach

Parties climbing South Tahoma Glacier Headwall, Success Cleaver and Success Finger usually approach via Success Divide. Hike to Mirror Lakes via Indian Henry's Hunting Ground, then skirt Pyramid Peak on the left side to Success Divide. There are bivouac sites at several places along the divide. Mirror Lakes and Pyramid Peak are heavily-impacted areas, so use no-trace techniques when passing through this area. The following routes are commonly reached via this approach:

The **South Tahoma Glacier** route (④; 10-12 hrs) climbs the South Tahoma Glacier through its headwall to Point Success. Drop down to the glacier and ascend as crevasses permit to the bergschrund deep within the cirque. The headwall has reportedly been climbed by three distinct routes. Early season only; rockfall and avalanche danger. Grade III.

Mount Rainier

The **Success Cleaver** route (③; 10-12 hrs) follows the long ridge descending from Point Success on the southwest. Approach either from Longmire or Kautz Creek Trail to Indian Henry's Hunting Ground. Traverse around the left side of Pyramid Peak onto lower Success Cleaver. Ascend cinder slopes on the cleaver's crest until forced down and right onto the Success Glacier Headwall. Continue up snow or ice slopes between rock bands to where the cleaver merges with Kautz Cleaver and continue to Point Success. Popular only because it doesn't involve glacier travel, but very long. Rockfall hazard. Grade II.

To ascend the **Success Glacier Headwall** route (③; 10-12 hrs), begin on Success Divide and descend right of Success Cleaver onto Pyramid Glacier. Cross the ridge dividing Pyramid and Success Glaciers and contour up the Success Glacier to the headwall. Ascend the rightmost of the three broad couloirs (the "Success Finger") to Kautz Cleaver. Grade II, rockfall and avalanche hazard.

A view of Mount Rainier's west side.

Photo: Austin Post, U. S. Geological Survey

Wapowety Cleaver Approach

The Kautz Cleaver and Kautz Headwall routes begin from Wapowety Cleaver, which is commonly approached via Van Trump Park Trail and the Van Trump Glaciers. A longer approach goes along the ridge crest above Mildred Point. Most parties bivouac on the cleaver (several good sites) and cross the Kautz Glacier on the morning of their ascent. Stay on snow as much as possible to minimize your impact in this sensitive area. Do not construct new campsites on bare ground. Two routes can be approached from here:

The **Kautz Cleaver** route (③; 10-12 hrs) ascends the rock spur separating the Success and Kautz glaciers. Approach from Christine Falls and Van Trump Park, or from Mirror Lakes via Success Glacier. Cross the Kautz Glacier above the icefall at about 9,000 feet to the base of Kautz Cleaver, and ascend the cleaver via snow gullies and slopes past a prominent rock tower on the right. Continue toward Point Success. Grade III. Rockfall hazard.

The increasingly popular **Kautz Glacier Headwall** route ★ (②; 8-10 hrs) climbs the headwall above the lower portion of the Kautz Glacier, immediately right of the Kautz Cleaver. Ascend the Wapowety Cleaver to about 10,000 feet. Traverse onto the glacier and ascend the snow finger up the headwall to where rock bands must be passed (Class 3) or avoided to reach Point Success. Grade III. Rockfall and avalanche hazard.

Camp Hazard Approach

The Kautz Glacier and Wilson Glacier Headwall routes begin from Paradise. Ascend the Skyline Trail to Glacier Vista, and descend to the Nisqually Glacier. Cross the glacier as crevasses allow to a prominent gully dividing cliffs on the far side. Ascend this gully to the left edge of the Wilson Glacier. Continue up and left along the glacier's edge, ascending snowfields (several possibilities) on the east side of Wapowety Cleaver. The camp is merely a flat spot on the ridge. The camp is named for early explorer and writer Joseph Hazard, and not because it is in a precarious position. Three routes (Wilson Glacier Headwall, Fuhrer Thumb and Fuhrer Finger) use this approach.

It is possible to reach Camp Hazard from Van Trump Park, but this involves more distance and elevation gain than the approach from Paradise and is not as popular.

Camp Hazard has serious sanitation problems. Do everything possible to minimize your impact in this area.

Kautz Glacier ★ ② 4-6 hrs

This route was the approximate line attempted by Lt. August V. Kautz in 1857. Kautz and party are credited with attaining nearly 13,000 feet in elevation. The route was frequently used by guided parties after the collapse of Gibraltar Ledge in 1936, until the Disappointment Cleaver route gained popularity.

From Camp Hazard, descend slightly onto the Kautz Glacier, skirt the ice cliff area and climb a steep ice chute connecting the lower and upper Kautz Glacier. The route under the ice cliff is not usually unsafe, but move fast anyway. Continue as conditions permit to the summit plateau. A large crevasse above 12,000 feet may require skirting on the west side after July.

Mount Rainier

Mount Rainier's southwest face.

Photo: Austin Post, U.S. Geological Survey

Depending upon conditions, it may be possible to climb over the ice cliff, and rappel over the cliff on the descent. However, be on guard against falling ice. This may save time, but it is more risky. The ice cliff was climbed easily in the early 1940s, but has become a very imposing wall in recent years. Ice screws are recommended for the chute, which can be tricky, especially on the way down.

Fuhrer Finger ★ ② 4-6 hrs

This is considered the fastest route to the summit of Mount Rainier, and is sometimes climbed in one day round trip from Paradise. It was first climbed by guides Hans and Heinie Fuhrer, with Joseph Hazard and others, in 1920. In August 1934, park ranger Bill

Butler made a round trip from Paradise to the summit in 11 hours, 20 minutes (a time which has since been beaten by several others).

Ascend from Paradise across the Nisqually Glacier and to the left side of the Wilson Glacier, or ascend the Nisqually Glacier to where you can traverse directly across to the base of the finger (a less-avalanche-prone approach for early season). Continue into the obvious snow finger on the right side of the upper Wilson Glacier, and up to the upper Nisqually Glacier. From the top of the finger, ascend along the upper left margin of the Nisqually Glacier, or directly if feasible.

Beware of killer avalanches down the chute, especially in late spring. Glissading down the chute is not recommended for safety reasons. Rockfall is likely. After August, the Finger becomes unsafe.

A variation (**Fuhrer Thumb**) ascends the prominent couloir between the Wilson Glacier Headwall and Fuhrer Finger. It is steeper and narrower than Fuhrer Finger, and has more rockfall hazard. The couloir is split at the bottom by rock outcroppings, permitting variations. Both Fuhrer Thumb variations eventually connect with the Fuhrer Finger route. A bergschrund may present a problem later in the year. Grade III.

Other South Side Summit Routes

The **Wilson Glacier Headwall** route (③; 6-8 hrs) climbs ice chutes through the headwall above Wilson Glacier, and, like Fuhrer Finger, is a direct route to the summit in early season. Ascend from Paradise as for the Kautz Glacier route. Ascend a snow finger and ice chutes on the left side of the headwall, left of a prominent rock buttress. Continue to the crest and across the summit plateau to the crater rim. Beware of falling ice from the Kautz ice cliffs, and of avalanches. In later season, a rock step has to be negotiated (Class 4). Rockfall and icefall hazard. Grade III.

The **Nisqually Glacier Icefall** route (④; 4-6 hrs) ascends the steep and heavily-fractured Nisqually Glacier as it is squeezed down from the summit ice plateau. Traverse down and left from Camp Muir to the center of the Nisqually Glacier and ascend the icefall as is practical, depending upon serac conditions. This route has significant icefall and rockfall danger, particularly while passing below the ice cliff and Gibraltar Chute, and while below the icefall. Grade III.

The **Nisqually Glacier Ice Cliff** route (④; 4-6 hrs) ascends the eastern lobe of the upper Nisqually Glacier, passing an immense ice cliff. Descend from Camp Muir around Cowlitz Cleaver, then up the Nisqually Glacier to the ice cliff. Ascend a chute on the extreme left side of the ice cliff (and not the ice cliff proper) onto the upper glacier. Nobody has yet ascended the ice cliff proper; the chute permits relatively safe passage. Rockfall and icefall danger. Grade III. Rockfall and icefall hazard.

Other variations include ascending the upper Nisqually Cleaver, climbing Nisqually Cleaver directly from its base, and heading up the Gibraltar Chute, all of which have horribly loose rock and great exposure to rock or icefall. These are rarely climbed and are not especially recommended.

Little Tahoma Peak rises on the left, with Mount Rainier in the background.

Photo: Rob Lovitt

Chapter Five:
Little Tahoma Peak

Little Tahoma Peak is a craggy remnant of the once-higher Mount Rainier volcano. It is largely unstable, and is being undercut by glaciers on both sides, particularly by the Emmons Glacier. In 1963, a massive rockfall occurred on the peak's north face, scattering debris on the glacier below and obliterating the only route climbed on that face so far.

Although a mere satellite peak of Mount Rainier, Little Tahoma, at 11,138 ft./3395m, stands taller than most other summits in the Cascade Range. It is a popular ascent, mostly because of its elevation, and it's only recommended route is easy. Little Tahoma is not recommended for inexperienced climbers or scramblers because it requires glacier travel and has very loose rock. The Fryingpan and Whitman Glaciers are popular with telemark skiers.

A climbing card is required for ascents of Little Tahoma Peak. Roping up on the glaciers is advised.

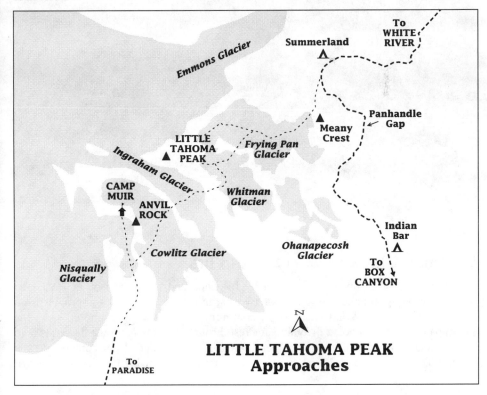

LITTLE TAHOMA PEAK Approaches

Little Tahoma Peak

Little Tahoma Peak and Mount Rainier. Photo: Austin Post, U. S. Geological Survey

Whitman Glacier ★ ① 6-8 hrs

This route was taken on the first ascent by J.B. Flett and H.H. Garrison in 1895. The route may be approached by either of two variations. Most parties approach from Summerland via the Wonderland Trail, continuing to Meany Crest and crossing the Fryingpan Glacier to a notch in Whitman Crest. From the notch, the route descends onto the Whitman Glacier and joins the other approach, which comes from Paradise via the Skyline Trail (as for Camp Muir), but breaks off across the Cowlitz Glacier below Anvil

Little Tahoma Peak

Rock. This variation continues across the Ingraham Glacier and reaches the Whitman Glacier via a broad gap in the east ridge of Little Tahoma. Because of time, complexity and greater crevasse danger, the Summerland approach is recommended (unless you are already at Camp Muir).

The route ascends the Whitman Glacier to its head, then follows snow or loose rock to a short traverse left that gives access to several hundred feet of snow or loose rock. The summit is reached by a final short scramble (very loose but easy).

Other Summit Routes

The **Northeast Face** route (④; 10-12 hrs) rises above the head of the Fryingpan Glacier. Approach from Summerland. The route climbs the face above the head of the glacier, eventually traversing right around the summit formation. The first-ascent party reached the summit pinnacle by passing the right skyline pinnacle on the north and ascending a difficult steep rock pitch just east of the pinnacle, then traversing about 300 feet across loose "shingle" rock to a notch, where three consecutive rotten rock pillars were climbed directly to the summit. Rockfall hazard. Grade IV, Class 5.

The **North Face** route (⑤; 6-8 hrs) was climbed in 1959, but never repeated. In 1963, a massive rockfall destroyed much of the route and left the face highly unstable. No attempts have been reported since the first ascent. Even then, it was considered a suicide route. Rockfall hazard. Those wishing to push their luck should first refer to *The Challenge of Rainier* or the *Cascade Alpine Guide* Vol. 1.

The spiny **West Ridge** (⑤; 12+ hrs) of Little Tahoma was considered the last unclimbed natural line on Mount Rainier. The first ascent was made during winter conditions to avoid loose rock. The route is approached most easily via Cathedral Gap from Camp Muir. The first-ascent party bypassed loose rock via difficult, poorly-protected ice climbing, with 18 belayed pitches and three rappels off gendarmes. Like the **Northeast Face** route, the route followed will be dictated by prevailing conditions. This route should not be climbed except when thoroughly coated with ice. Grade V, Class 5. Rockfall hazard.

Mount St. Helens on May 18, 1980.

Photo: Robert M. Kimmell, U.S. Geological Survey

Chapter Six:
Mount St. Helens
Washington, 8,365 ft./2550m

Mount St. Helens hardly needs an introduction here. The present mountain is a poor reminder of the once-symetrical cone rising above the placid waters of Spirit Lake. Though named for a friend of Captain George Vancouver, the native name "Low-We-Lat-Klah" or "Low-We-Not-Thlat" (or "Loowit"), meaning "Throwing-Up-Smoke" or "Smoking Mountain," is more apt.

The formerly-interesting summit climb, too, has been reduced to a strenuous tourist hike by the now-legendary eruption. The pre-eruption volcano rose to a height of 9,677 ft./2950m, and was first ascended by Thomas J. Dryer, founder of *The Oregonian,* and his party, in 1853. Post-1980 ascents were made prior to the opening of the "Red Zone," and a few parties were arrested and fined for their derring-do. The first post-eruption ascent was probably made during the winter of 1981-82; illegal ascents were certainly made during spring 1982 and after. The first legal post-eruption ascent of Mount St. Helens was not made until 1987.

Most visitors to Mount St. Helens prior to 1980 thought impossible the eventual eruption that blew off more than 1,000 feet of the mountain's summit and devastated the surrounding landscape. The mountain had not been active during the previous century, aside from a few long-forgotten outbursts of steam and ash, and there was no evidence to the casual observer that the mountain was active. Geologists, however, had from 1975 predicted a possible violent eruption in the near future.

In March 1980, the mountain gave its first sign in 123 yearsof awaking with an earthquake measuring more than 4.0 on the Richter Scale. The earthquakes continued, growing stronger and more frequent, until harmonic tremors occurred almost continuously without pause. The mountain swelled and its crater opened. Mount St. Helens was poised and ready for a big eruption. Still, life went on as if nothing unusual were happening. Geologists flew daily reconnaisance over the mountain, and Harry Truman refused to budge from his Spirit Lake lodge even after evacuation of the "Red Zone" was ordered.

"Where were you when the mountain blew?" In the quiet of early morning on May 18, 1980, an earthquake registering 5.0 on the Richter Scale caused an enormous landslide, as the north side of Mount St. Helens collapsed and slid toward Spirit Lake. This collapse literally uncorked the pressure that had built up within the mountain, causing upward and outward explosions of gas, ash and pyroclastic projectiles that killed everything within a one- kilometer radius of the north side of the mountain (the "Eruption Impact Area"), and shot an ash cloud 14 miles into the stratosphere.

Mount St. Helens

Pyroclastic material as hot as 1,600° Farenheit poured down the mountain at speeds estimated at 100 miles per hour, cushioned by compressed air, burning everything that was left intact after the eruption. Water from displaced lakes, mixed with ash, snow, ice and assorted volcanic debris, generated catastrophic mud flows that wiped out bridges, logging equipment and buildings.

This brief account of the events of May 18 and the days to follow hardly captures the eruption of Mount St. Helens in all its glory. If you wish to learn more about historical or geological Mount St. Helens, please consult the bibliography and its references, visit the visitor's center, view any of dozens of films chronicling the eruption – or better yet, visit the northern portion of the monument to get a firsthand look at the destructive legacy of the May 1980 eruption. If you visit the mountain, you will see that the barren wilderness created by the eruption is slowly coming back to life.

As noted previously, the climb to the summit of Mount St. Helens is no longer challenging, but it is certainly much more popular. The Forest Service estimates the number of post-eruption ascents at about 12,000 as of September 1987. Permits are reserved months in advance for the climb. Don't expect solitude here.

While there are several possible ways to climb the mountain, the usual route is via Monitor Ridge, which reaches the summit fairly directly. Other routes have been climbed since the eruption, and others may be possible, but none is truly technical in a mountaineering sense. Early-season ascents are recommended, as snow climbing is usually preferable to slogging up endless steep pumice slopes. Tourists and casual hikers probably will want to wait until after the snow is gone before climbing the mountain, unless they are prepared for steep snow travel.

Climbers should be wary of the crater rim, which is quite unstable and prone to avalanching. Keep back! Be sure to bring sun and wind protection, and gaiters and goggles to keep ash out of your boots and eyes. Ice axes, crampons and ropes are advisable as conditions require them.

Permits are required for all travel above timberline. From November 1 to May 14, simply register before and after your climb at Jack's Restaurant, which is located 5 miles west of Cougar on Route 503. Between May 15 and October 31, permits are issued on a first-come, first-served basis, so come early. Beginning in February, mail-in applications to monument headquarters are accepted, and 70 permits per day are issued by this process. An additional 40 permits are issued from Jack's Restaurant (see monument information provided below). Permits go fast, so get yours early! Permits are valid for 36 hours, allowing overnight camping prior to the ascent. Climbers must sign in and check out.

Because Mount St. Helens has no technical climbing to offer, only two routes will be described. If you intend to try a different route, please do so when it is snow-covered; late-season ascents undoubtedly will damage the "fragile" slopes of Mount St. Helens, and human-caused erosion should be minimized.

For more information about climbing Mount St. Helens, contact:

Mt. St. Helens National Volcanic Monument (206) 247-5473
Rt. 1, Box 369
Amboy, WA 98601

Mount St. Helens 87

Before . . .

and after.

Photos: (top) Austin Post; (bottom) Robert M. Kimmell, both of U. S. Geological Survey

Don't forget Mount. St. Helens is an *active* volcano. Even though geologists can better predict eruptions, an eruption could still occur without much warning. The lava dome is still growing, and has blown off several times already. In the event of an eruption, descend immediately, avoiding gullies and depressions, and breathe through a moist cloth if ash overwhelms you.

Rating details appear on pages 4 through 7 of the Introduction.

Forest Service Road Approaches

To reach the routes, drive about 4 miles past Cougar on Highway 90. Turn left onto Forest Service Road 83 soon after the Highway 90 bends north to skirt Swift Reservoir. Drive about three miles to the road fork (it become unpaved here); take the left fork, which is Forest Service Road 81. After about 1.5 mi, turn right onto Forest Service Road 830 to Monitor Ridge, and follow that road 2 mi to the trailhead. To reach Butte Camp, continue up Forest Service Road 81 1.5 mi to the trailhead for Toutle Trail 238.

Monitor Ridge   (0)   5-7 hrs

Ptarmigan Trail (Forest Service #216A) leads two gradual uphill miles to Loowit Trail 216, at timberline. From there, the "trail" continues more or less directly up lava flows and levees to the low ridge. The route is supposed to be marked with poles for easy routefinding. Attain a saddle between the true summit and a false summit. The true summit is about .25 mi west, an easy traverse along the ash-covered rim. Again, beware of landslides and cornices on the crater rim.

Butte Camp   (0)   5 hrs

Hike .75 mi up Toutle Trail 238 to a junction; go right on Butte Camp Trail 238A another 1.75 mi to Butte Camp (4,000 feet), where you'll find the last water and a popular campsite. Continue 1 mi to Loowit Trail 216. Climb easy slopes to the summit rim. This is a good spring route, but after the snow melts, it becomes a steep pumice slog and is not recommended.

Mount St. Helens

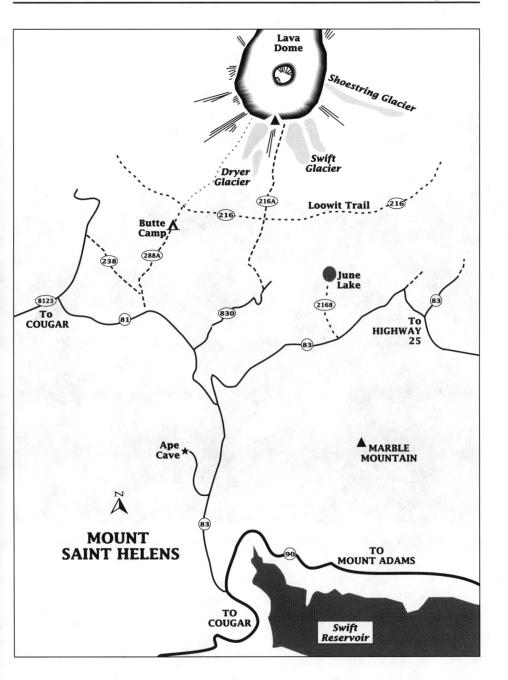

Roosevelt Cliff on Mount Adams.

Photo: Austin Post, U.S. Geological Survey

Chapter Seven:
Mount Adams
Washington, 12,276 ft./3742m

The third highest of the Cascade volcanoes, Mount Adams ("Washington's forgotten volcano") rises above the rounded foothills of the eastern Cascade range, much farther east than its neighboring volcanoes. Adams is the second most-massive volcano of the Cascade Range, about one-third larger than Mount Rainier. It is not a precipitous peak, but a broad dacite dome.

The mountain was observed by Lewis and Clark's expedition in 1805, and was mistaken for St. Helens. Later explorers and cartographers frequently confused the two mountains. In 1839, the mountain officially was named for President John Adams as part of Hall Kelley's "President's Range" scheme to rename all of the volcanoes down the coast after U.S. presidents. This plan had limited success, as Adams apparently was the only peak named under this scheme, and this by a cartographer's error. Although botanist David Douglas was said to have climbed the mountain shortly after his arrival in the region in 1825, the first ascent of Mount Adams is credited to an 1854 party, including A.G. Aiken, E.J. Allen, Andrew Birge and B.F. Shaw. For a time, there was a manned lookout cabin atop Mount Adams, which was built with the help of horse and mule pack trains. The ruins of the lookout still stand, supported by a mass of old snow inside the frame. For a brief time, a sulphur mine operated at the summit, but was abandoned when it proved unprofitable.

Mount Adams is not typical of the Cascade volcanoes. It lacks the symmetry of Hood and Shasta and the abruptness of Rainier. It stands so far east of the Cascade crest that it is readily visible only from the summits of nearby volcanoes and the Hood River Gorge region. Although believed to have erupted from a single vent, several lateral eruptions high on the main cone have spread the mountain out. Adams was originally thought to be a long ridge composed of several cones which erupted at different times to produce the large mass that is the mountain today, and not a single mountain extruded from a single vent or cone, which has been more recently theorized. Although a single-vent volcano will typically produce a more uniform, symmetrical volcanic shape, such as St. Helens or Hood, this apparently has not been the case with Mount Adams.

The mountain is believed to have begun forming about half a million years ago, with the most recent cone building within the last 25,000 years. Geologists suspect the mountain is almost entirely composed of dark andesite, which is a bit more resistant to erosion than other volcanic materials. The mountain has displayed little evidence of its volcanic birth during the past two hundred years, other than by its summit fumaroles, but has been subject to other geological events, most notably large rockfalls similar to that which recently occurred on Mount Rainier's Russell Cliff. Continued volcanic activity is thought unlikely, but Mount Adams is very prone to future rockfalls and mudslides.

Mount Adams

> For information about access and permits, contact:
>
> Mt. Adams Ranger District (509) 395-2501
> Trout Lake, WA 98650

Like that of other Cascade volcanoes, the rock of Mount Adams is usually rotten or unstable. Few routes climb over any significant rock obstacle, but stick to snow and ice as much as possible, and for good reason. Rockfall is a hazard on many of Mount Adams' routes, particularly its headwalls, where nearly every climbing party has dodged significant rockfall. Most headwall routes on Mount Adams remain mostly unrepeated, for good reason. Future climbers may become desperate enough to attempt to climb the several rotten headwalls of Mount Adams, but let us hope they have more sense.

Mount Adams is situated partially within the Mount Adams Wilderness, and partially within the Yakima Indian Reservation. A Yakima tribal-use permit is needed if you drive into the "Tract-D" area (Bird Creek Meadows) on the southeast side. This permit can be obtained from the Mt. Adams Ranger District office, and must be displayed when parked at the trailhead. There is a self-service registration box at the ranger station for use after hours and on weekends. For more information, refer to *Cascade Alpine Guide Vol. 1*.

Rating details appear on pages 4 through 7 of the Introduction.

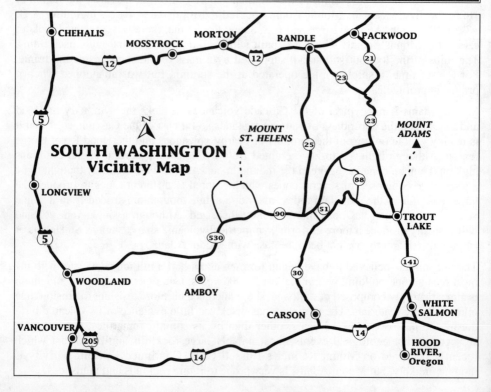

SOUTH WASHINGTON Vicinity Map

Cold Springs Approach

The South Spur and Avalanche Glacier routes are commonly approached from Cold Springs Campground, which is reached from Trout Lake via Forest Service Road 8040 (the turnoff is well-marked as "Mount Adams Recreation Area;" follow the signs). Mazama Glacier also may be reached from the campground, although most parties prefer the shorter and more direct route from Bird Creek Meadows.

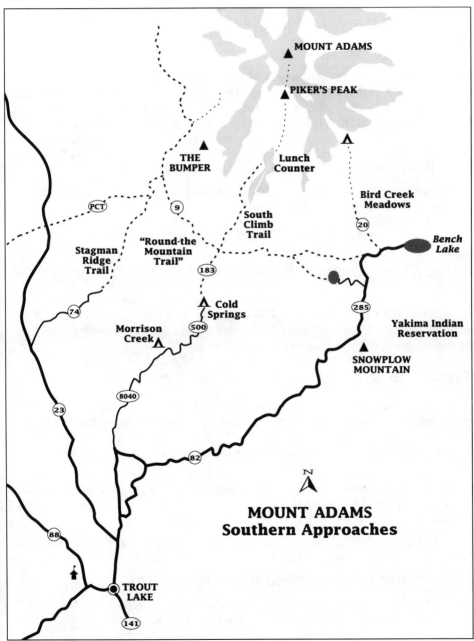

MOUNT ADAMS Southern Approaches

South Spur ★ ⓪ 6-8 hrs 🐎

"You are a piker if you think this is the summit. Don't crab, the mountain was here first." Inscription on rock at false summit ("Piker's Peak").

The South Spur is the most popular and least technical route on the mountain. Mules made the ascent on a regular basis during the mining era. Hike South Climb Trail 183 to the left edge of the tiny Crescent Glacier and on to the "Lunch Counter," a flat area at about 9,000 feet. Ascend Suksdorf Ridge to the false summit (11,657 ft.). Continue across a gentle saddle to the true summit.

The route is easy, with no special difficulty or danger, except possibly avalanches in early season. Although the route does cross the summit icecap, if you stay on the route, crevasses are not a problem. Bring crampons and ice axes, and a rope. Glissading is the most popular method of descent, but should not be attempted when snowcover is insufficient to provide a safe runout. Some parties camp at the Lunch Counter, although the round trip is feasible from Cold Springs if you start early. This is a popular ski descent in early summer.

An alternate approach follows Round-the-Mountain Trail 9 east to McDonald Ridge, which is traversed directly north to the Lunch Counter.

Bird Creek Meadows Approach

Most of the southeast-side routes of Mount Adams are approached from Bird Creek Meadows. This requires access to the Yakima Indian Reservation, and a Tract-D Permit (available from the wilderness ranger or the Forest Service office). Drive Forest Service Roads 8290 and 285 to Bird Creek Meadows Trail 20. From trail's end, continue cross-country to the head of the Hellroaring Creek drainage, then follow moraine slopes to the toe of the Mazama Glacier. Continue to Mazama Glacier Saddle ("Sunrise Camp"), the popular bivouac site. Route descriptions begin from here.

Mazama Glacier ★ ① 5-7 hrs

The Mazama Glacier flanks the south spur on the east. It is a good, basic glacier climb and is popular. An approach can be made via two likely routes. It is possible to hike east from the South Climb Trail 183/Round-the-Mountain Trail 9 junction to Bird Creek Meadows, but it is shorter to begin from Bird Creek Meadows.

The route ascends the right flank of the Mazama Glacier to the South Spur. There are no special difficulties, although there is frequent rockfall from the right side of the Mazama Glacier at about 9,000 feet. Crevasses can be a problem in late season. Cornices frequently form on Suksdorf Ridge.

A direct finish variation up the headwall takes you more directly to Piker's Peak. This involves a steep (60°) ice slope. Grade II.

Other Routes Approached from the South

The **South Klickitat Glacier** route (④; 6-8 hrs), climbs the steep, narrow icefall on what is now considered the south lobe of the Klickitat Glacier. Descend from Mazama Glacier

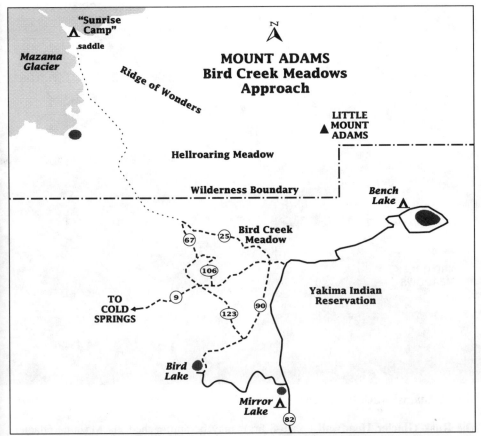

Saddle onto the south Klickitat Glacier, and ascend directly through the icefall (60° plus) to the south shoulder just below the false summit. Rockfall and icefall hazard. Grade III.

The **Klickitat Glacier** (④; 8-10 hrs) descends southeast from the summit slope through a narrow icefall into a broad glacial valley. Descend from Mazama Glacier Saddle and traverse to the middle of Klickitat Glacier as crevasses permit. The exact route up the glacier depends upon crevasse conditions. Rockfall, avalanche and icefall hazard. Grade III.

The **Klickitat Headwall** route (④; 8-10 hrs) climbs the major headwall dividing the lobes of the Klickitat Glacier. Drop down as for the Klickitat Glacier route, but ascend to the headwall. Serious rockfall danger, as well as avalanche and icefall hazard. Grade IV.

The **Castle** (⑤; 12+ hrs) is a prominent rock buttress at the head of Battlement Ridge, which divides the Rusk and Klickitat Glaciers. Approach via Mazama Glacier Saddle; traverse laterally across the Klickitat Glacier and over the crest of Battlement Ridge. Continue via the Rusk Glacier until it is feasible to regain the crest of Battlement Ridge. Approach the base of the Castle on the left side. Traverse right across snowfields (scree in late season) to a crumbly chimney on the northeast side; continue across The Castle and down to the Rusk Glacier, which is climbed to the summit. Rockfall hazard.

Mount Adams' Klickitat Glacier. Photo: Austin Post, U. S. Geological Survey

The **Rusk Glacier Headwall** (5; 6-8 hrs) may be approached via Mazama Glacier Saddle and Battlement Ridge. Ascend the Rusk Glacier to 40° snow-ice gullies on the right-central portion of the headwall. Ascend the gullies and Class 4 rock to the base of the ice cliff, which can be climbed directly, with five pitches of steep ice followed by a short ice overhang. Rockfall and icefall hazard; a "death route." Grade IV.

Killen Creek Approach

Approaches to most of the north and northeastern routes on Mount Adams begin on Killen Creek Trail 113. The trail leaves Forest Service Road 2329 just south of Killen Creek Camp. Follow the Killen Creek Trail to its junction with the PCT, where Killen Meadows Trail 110 leads to Killen Meadows. From trail's end, your direction depends on which route you are climbing. Camping in Killen Meadows is popular but often crowded and environmentally destructive. Bivouacking higher up, on snow or ice, is suggested to reduce impacts on Killen Meadows. Most of the following route descriptions for begin from the Killen Meadows trail junction. The Killen Creek approach is most popular for Wilson, Lyman and Lava Glaciers, and Lava and North Ridges. Victory Ridge also may be reached this way, although it is equidistant from Bird Creek Meadows.

More direct, but longer, hiking approaches to most eastside routes may be made via Muddy Meadows Trail 13. From Muddy Meadows, hike about 4.25 mi south to the

Mount Adams

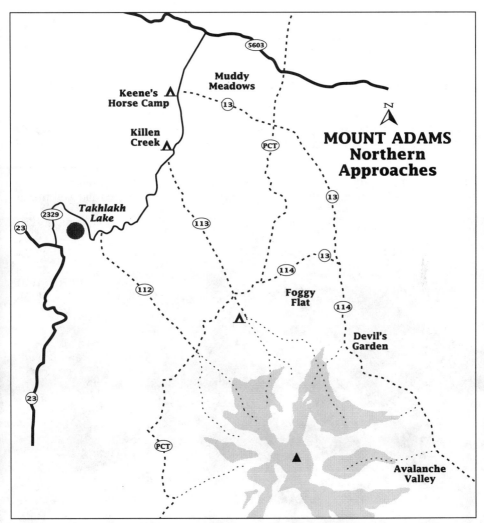

MOUNT ADAMS Northern Approaches

junction with Trail 114 (crossing the PCT at 2.5 mi along the way). Continue 5 mi south on Trail 114 to Devil's Gardens (very close to Lyman Glacier), then 2.5 mi to Avalanche Valley (which gives direct access to lower Victory Ridge, from which the Rusk and Wilson Glaciers are easily accessed). Because of the hiking distance, and because *Cascade Alpine Guide* recommends cross-country approaches from Killen Creek Trail, few use the eastside trail approaches. However, they do offer less cross-country travel and easier routefinding for routes on the east side of Mount Adams.

Adams Glacier ★ ④ 6-8 hrs

The Adams Glacier is the picturesque glacier descending northwest from the summit ice cap in an impressive icefall. It is highly regarded as a Mount Adams classic. From Killen Creek Trail, 1 mi of cross-country hiking leads to the lower slope of the Adams Glacier. The route is pretty straightforward, ascending whichever path you find through the steep crevasse jumble. The angle remains between 40° and 50°. Most parties begin on the right and finish on the left, although any route is possible so long as crevasses permit. Ascents prior to August are customary; later on, the glacier becomes badly crevassed. Grade III.

Lava Ridge 6-8 hrs

Lava Ridge is the cleaver dividing the Lava and Lyman glaciers. Approach via Killen Creek, crossing the North Ridge onto Lava Glacier, or via cross-country hiking over the Lava Glacier moraine from Trail 114. Ascend the obvious ridge at or near its crest until it fades into a rounded ice slope. Continue to the summit icecap and to the summit.

There are no notable difficulties during optimal conditions. It is a long route, with loose rock, and is not very popular, But it is a good climb when snow-covered and well-frozen.

Lava Ridge and surrounding routes. Photo: Austin Post, U. S. Geological Survey.

Other Routes Approached from the North

Numerous other routes can be approached from the north via the Killen Creek approach. Moving counterclockwise around the mountain:

The **Wilson Glacier Headwall – Victory Ridge** route (5; 8-10 hrs) is considered a "death route." Victory Ridge is a sharp spur dividing the Rusk and Wilson Glaciers. Climb the southernmost lobe of Wilson Glacier, staying well right of Victory Ridge's crumbly flanks. No one has climbed rotten Victory Ridge directly; the route parallels it on the Wilson Glacier side, eventually climbing the central ice couloir (4-5 pitches, 55° mixed climbing) of the Wilson Glacier headwall. Exit left via a long traverse beneath the ice cliff to upper Rusk Glacier. Some parties have found this an icy, enjoyable, albeit scary ascent. Rockfall and icefall hazard. Grade IV.

The **Wilson Glacier** route (④; 8-10 hrs) has two variations, both of which are serious undertakings. The icefall route ascends left of rock formations to the narrow icefall, where the glacier is squeezed between two rock cliffs. Grade II. The headwall route goes a bit farther left on the Wilson Glacier, and ascends slopes immediately right of a prominent cleaver dividing the lower Wilson Glacier. Continue to Roosevelt Cliff, passing the bergschrund and climbing a rockfall funnel (i.e., gully) to the upper slopes. Skirt around the ice cliffs to the upper glacier. Rockfall and icefall hazard. Grade III.

The **Lyman Glacier** (④; 8-10 hrs) descends from the summit icecap contiguous with the Wilson Glacier, but is cleaved off and again divided into two sections. The north route ascends obliquely across the glacier from the toe of Lava Ridge. Continue up the narrow icefall between the Lyman Cleaver and Lava Ridge. Grade II. The south route stays low on the glacier, until past a cleaver dividing the lobes of the Lyman Glacier, then ascends fairly directly up the narrow glacier as crevasses and seracs permit. Icefall hazard. Grade III.

The **Lava Glacier** (③; 6-8 hrs) has two variations through the steep headwall that fronts the glacier. Both are nearly identical, crossing the bergschrund and climbing the headwall. Serious rockfall and avalanche danger; a "death route." Grade III, Class 4.

The **North Ridge** route (①; 8 hrs) is a simple ascent, but because of its length and loose rock, is not entirely popular. Avoid a few minor obstacles on your way to the summit shoulder. A long hike on the icecap leads to the summit dome. Rockfall hazard. Class 2. Typically done as a traverse, descending the south slope.

The **Headwall Variation** of the **North Ridge** route (③; 8-10 hrs) begins up an obvious snowfield right of the ridge, and continues up snow gullies and scree slopes to the right to a higher chute that leads to the summit icecap. Serious rockfall and avalanche hazard. Grade III, Class 4.

The **Stormy Monday Couloir** route (④; 8-10 hrs) follows the large northwest-face couloir immediately left of the Adams Glacier icefall. Ascend the couloir to a rock band (or two) that reaches a sickle-shaped 50° ice gully. Climb the steep, narrow gully to the summit shoulder. Rockfall and avalanche danger. Grade III, Class 4 or 5.

The **Northwest Ridge** route (③; 8-10 hrs) is named for the ridge that divides the Adams and Pinnacle Glaciers. Like many of the ridges on Mount Adams, it is not technically difficult, just long and loose. Approach as for the Adams Glacier. Gain the ridge via snowfields just above its toe, and ascend the ridge. Continue to the West Peak and traverse to the summit. Rockfall hazard. Class 2.

The **Adams Glacier to Northwest Ridge** variation (6-8 hrs) is a steep (averaging over 50°), somewhat popular variation that ascends from the Adams Glacier directly to the West Peak via snow and ice slopes. Grade III.

The Adams Glacier and environs. Photo: Austin Post, U. S. Geological Survey

The **Pinnacle Glacier Headwall** route (③; 8-10 hrs) climbs the cirque between the West and Northwest Ridges. The customary approach is as for the West Ridge, crossing into the Pinnacle Glacier cirque when feasible. Once on the glacier, ascend the right portion of the headwall, via snow slopes and gullies, to the West Ridge. Serious rockfall and avalanche danger. Grade II, Class 4.

The **West Ridge** route (①; 8-10 hrs) ascends the gentle ridge separating the Pinnacle and White Salmon Glaciers. The shortest approach heads up Stagman Ridge Trail 12 to Horseshoe Meadow (4.75 miles), then goes about 1 mi north on the PCT. Alternatively, hike the PCT from Swampy Meadows to Horseshoe Meadow. From the PCT, ascend cross-country to the ridge crest. Follow the ridge until it joins the Northwest Ridge, and continue to the summit. Rockfall hazard. Class 2.

Mount Adams 101

The **White Salmon – Avalanche Glacier** route (①; 6-8 hrs) is not the easiest on the mountain, but it is fairly direct. Approach from Cold Springs Campground. Hike South Climb Trail 183 to timberline, then follow the contour north cross-country to the terminus of Avalanche Glacier. Ascend north on Avalanche Glacier until it merges into the White Salmon Glacier cirque. Continue to the gap between the Pinnacle ("West Peak") and the summit, then to the summit. Rockfall and avalanche hazard.

The **Southwest Chute** route (①; 6-8 hrs) ascends a snow chute directly to the south summit. Approach as for the Avalanche Glacier, then ascend the snow chute or one of its neighbors. Don't try it when avalanche conditions are high, or after snow has melted away, or you'll be dodging bullets all the way to the top. Rockfall and avalanche hazard.

The White Salmon and Avalanche Glaciers spill down the west side of Mount Adams.

Photo: Austin Post, U. S. Geological Survey

Mount Hood, Oregon's highest volcano.

Photo: Alan Kearney

Chapter Eight:
Mount Hood
Oregon, 11,239 ft./3426m

Standing at more than 11,000 feet only 50 miles east of Portland, Mount Hood dominates the Columbia River Gorge and most of northwestern Oregon in the same way Mount Rainier commands the view from Puget Sound and Mount Shasta from northern California. Mount Hood is considered a dormant volcano, having not erupted since 1907, though it has active fumaroles in its crater. The mountain has had some relatively minor eruptions in the past 200 to 300 years, but is not believed to have demonstrated any major volcanic activity for at least 1,000 years. The mountain is estimated to have reached a height of just over 12,000 feet, but steady erosion, glaciation and unstable composition have conspired to wear it down to its present height and form. Minor lava flows have occurred within the unrecorded past, but these were from lateral vents and not from the summit crater. Given its accessibility, Mount Hood's south side is an excellent geological field study, having numerous exposed volcanic and glacial features, including moraines, plug domes, flows and deposits of varying composition, and thermal vents. Geologists agree that Mount Hood is among the most likely Pacific Northwest Coast volcanoes to erupt in the future.

Mount Hood has a long and interesting climbing history. The first accepted ascent of Mount Hood was by W.S. Buckley, W.L. Chittenden, James Deardorff, H.L. Pittock and L.J. Powell in 1857. Thomas Dryer, Oregonian editor and Mount St. Helens first-ascentionist, claimed an ascent in 1854, but faulty route descriptions discredited his claim. Regardless of who made the first climb, thousands followed. Climbing parties of more than 100 became common around the turn of the century. The Mazamas club of Portland was formed on the summit in 1894, when 193 climbers made the ascent. Although climbing parties of more than 20 are less common these days, it is not rare for more than 100 climbers to visit the summit on early-summer weekend days.

Because of its commanding position from Portland, the Columbia River Gorge and most of north central Oregon, Mount Hood is a much-revered and sought-after summit. Although it has been called the most-climbed glaciated peak in North America, Mount St. Helens likely has usurped that distinction since 1987, and South Sister, also glaciated, also is more-often climbed. Mount Hood is the most accessible of the "major" Cascade volcanoes. A year-round ski lift on its south slopes reaches to about 8,500 feet, and roads penetrate to timberline on two sides of the mountain, permitting hikes of less than one mile to glacier ice. Some of the climbing routes involve less than three miles of hiking/climbing. Many of Mount Hood's routes can be climbed in an easy day from timberline. Because of easy access to the standard routes, one-day round trips are common during late spring and summer. Because of its accessibility, Mount Hood's

Mount Hood

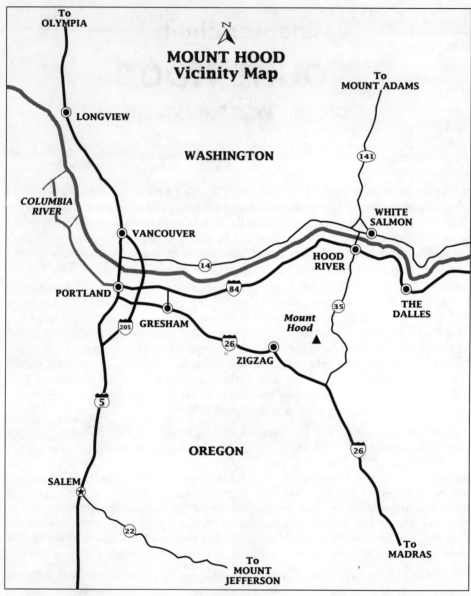

south side is the site of thousands of annual ascents. Climbers vie for the honor of being the first on top for each new year. Mount Hood reportedly has been ascended by a woman wearing high heels, and a bicycle has been ridden along the summit crest. A gibbon reached the summit in 1964. Dogs are frequent summit visitors.

Belying its pedestrian nature, Mount Hood has claimed many lives. In July 1956, the "Youth Hostel Accident" claimed the life of one youth and seriously injured 11 others. In May 1986, 11 died in another highly-publicized youth group accident. These and many other climbing accidents serve as reminders that Mount Hood is not an "easy climb" to be undertaken lightly. Still, many ill-prepared climbers and non-climbers head off from

Timberline Lodge bound for the summit. Fortunately, the summit is much farther away than it appears from Timberline, so most turn back. A few lucky fools do manage to reach the summit and return unharmed.

The culprit in most accidents on Mount Hood is the weather, which can be severe. Clear days often become cloudy, and storms can materialize with little warning. Cold temperatures, high winds and poor visibility have contributed to many fatalities and near-fatalities on Mount Hood. Once again, check the weather and avalanche reports before your climb, and heed rapid weather changes. Some parties have foolishly continued upward into a storm, becoming disoriented, lost and hypothermic. Equally to blame in many Mount Hood accidents is inexperience. The summit climb is not a hike, as some apparently believe. An ice axe and crampons are bare necessities here, no matter what the conditions, and even they may not be enough.

Climbers are encouraged to carry a special locator transmitter when climbing Mount Hood during uncertain weather. The transmitter, available for rent from local mountain shops, permits searchers to pinpoint a climber's exact location electronically when he or she becomes lost or stranded by bad weather, saving valuable search and rescue time. Contact the information officer at Zig Zag Ranger District office for details.

Most fatalities on Mount Hood result from the exercise of poor judgment by inexperienced climbers who overestimate their abilities and/or underestimate risks from effects of weather and other conditions. Proper planning, preparation and experience could have prevented many of these deaths. Inexperienced climbers should not try to climb Mount Hood unless in the company of an experienced leader or guide. Casual hikers on Mount Hood's upper slopes are frequent accident victims.

During poor weather, some climbers have become lost in the "Mount Hood Triangle" while descending the south side to Timberline. Unable to distinguish landmarks, they descend straight down, thinking they will come out at the lodge. Unfortunately, they find themselves far to the west, peering over the cliffs of Zig Zag Canyon. Taking a simple compass bearing during the ascent can save much time and trouble later. This is not a frequent problem, but one which still causes some concern. The Forest Service publishes a brochure that explains this phenomenon and provides other tips for staying on route during your descent. Read more about it at the day lodge before your climb.

As early as mid-July of most years, Mount Hood's routes are subjected to increasing rockfall, a serious hazard that is prevalent on all routes. Mount Hood's rock is quite simply awful. After May, and on warm days, try to get out of harm's way before 10 a.m. There is very little solid stone on Mount Hood, making any route passing beneath or over its "rock" very hazardous.

Self-registration is available at most trailheads. For further information, contact:

Zigzag Ranger District (503) 666-0704
70220 East Highway 224
Zigzag, OR 97049

Another hazard unrealized by a few climbers is the fumaroles. They smell pretty bad, like rotten eggs at best, so it's hard to believe anyone would want to get very close, but if you feel so inclined, think again. These vents are oxygen voids, a fact found out too late by at least one climber, who suffocated before he could get away.

One final note of interest – there is the year-round ski lift that operates from Timberline Lodge. The combined Palmer lifts climb just over 2,500 feet over snow and firn slopes between the Zigzag and Palmer Glaciers. Wise climbers stay clear of the ski slopes after the lift operation begins for the day. Skiing is Mount Hood's biggest attraction, bringing thousands of skiers and millions of dollars to its three commercial ski areas. Skiers "illuminate" the mountain in an annual event that is visible from Portland. Summer skiing on Palmer Glacier is very popular, and if you bring skis to the summit, you can sometimes enjoy a very long run from the crater down to Timberline Lodge.

Most of Mount Hood and the surrounding area is wilderness, protected by the Wilderness Act of 1964. The original wilderness was expanded to its present size in 1978. The entire mountain is not within the Wilderness boundary, as roads and ski lifts penetrate far up the mountain's south side. Climbers entering Mount Hood Wilderness are urged to use no-trace techniques to limit the visible signs of their use. Stay on snow whenever possible to protect fragile plant life and lessen erosion of loose pumice ridges. If staying overnight, pick a campsite that is sheltered from wind, but use existing sites or else camp on snow or ice. Don't displace rocks or soil to create new tent or bivouac sites. Human waste is a growing concern at high-use campsites; use minimum-impact human waste disposal methods. Don't cut switchbacks in the trails. Limit your party to no more than six climbers to lessen impacts caused by overuse. Come during the week to avoid overcrowding on popular routes. Clean up after yourself, and pack all refuse out. For more information on Mount Hood's routes, please see Jeff Thomas' *Oregon High* (Keep Climbing Press, 1991).

Rating details appear on pages 4 through 7 of the Introduction.

Timberline Lodge Approach

Most of the south- and west-side routes on Mount Hood originate from Timberline Lodge. The Depression-era lodge is a leading tourist attraction that also serves as a base for skiers using the year-round Palmer Lift.

The road leading to Timberline Lodge is well-marked, leaving Highway 26 a half-mile east of Government Camp. Five curvy miles lead upward to the lodge. Climbers are urged to register at the Wy'east Day Lodge on a voluntary basis; if you register, be sure to check out afterward. The climber registration "cave" provides route and other climber-oriented information. Registration soon will be mandatory, so get in the habit now. Camping is not allowed in the ski area parking lot; stay at the Forest Service campground just below.

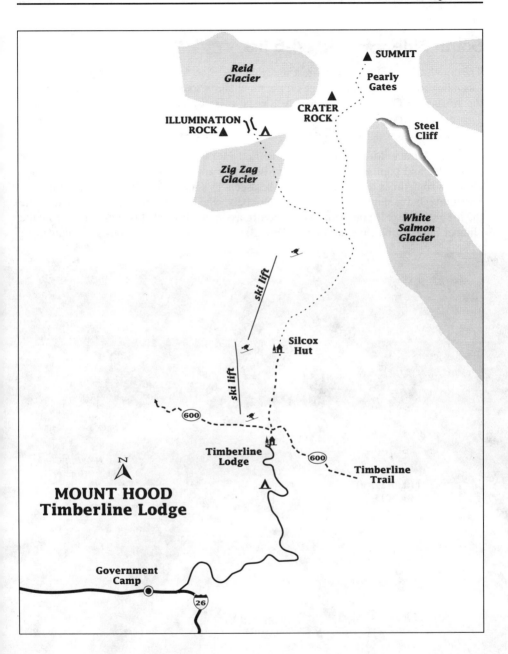

South Side ★ ① 4-6 hrs

The South Side route is the fastest and thus the most popular route on the mountain, ascending from Timberline Lodge on the mountain's south slope. Similar in character to the Avalanche Gulch route on Mount Shasta, it is straightforward and relatively short. This route deserves respect, particularly from inexperienced climbers. The route is often crowded, and slow parties regularly cause traffic jams above the bergschrund.

Hike "the Miracle Mile" from Timberline Lodge to the top of Palmer ski lift via littered snowfields and pumice ridges, passing Silcox Hut and debris from the ski area. Guided climbers sometimes hire a snowcat for the ascent to about 8,500 feet. Riding the lift is a possibility, but it starts too late for most climbers, who are on their way down by the time the lift gets going. If you want to ride the lift, ask at the lift-ticket booths across from the climber information cave at Wy'east Day Lodge. The ski area is an obstacle and danger

A view of the south side of Mount Hood. Photo: Austin Post, U. S. Geological Survey

Mount Hood

to climbers; avoid it if you can, particularly on the descent. But then, if you brought skis or a snowboard, cowabunga!

From the top of the east side of the ski slopes, climb snow slopes and a pumice ridge just above White River Glacier into the summit crater between Crater Rock and Steel Cliff, passing left of smelly Devil's Kitchen. Climb the "Hogback," a snow ridge above and behind Crater Rock, going as high as possible before encountering the bergschrund. The 'schrund is most often skirted on the right side. One of two snow chutes ("the Pearly Gates") around a short rotten wall gives access directly to the final summit slopes.

Beware of avalanches and rockfall below and in the Pearly Gates chute. Rockfall is the most common hazard here, especially after the sun hits the crater. The final slopes and gullies are sometimes very icy, making them quite treacherous.

When the Pearly Gates are plugged with slow climbers, some climbers use the "Old Crater" variation, climbing left from low on the Hogback to a broad, steep snow chute that meet the summit ridge a bit west of the summit. This variation is considered by some to be safer during periods of rockfall danger. Another route passes Crater Rock on the west side on the way to the Old Chute; this is steep, with higher rockfall danger.

Because this route is heavily-impacted, overnight camping is discouraged. The climb from Timberline takes only about 10 hours round trip, so bivouacking should not be necessary except in emergencies.

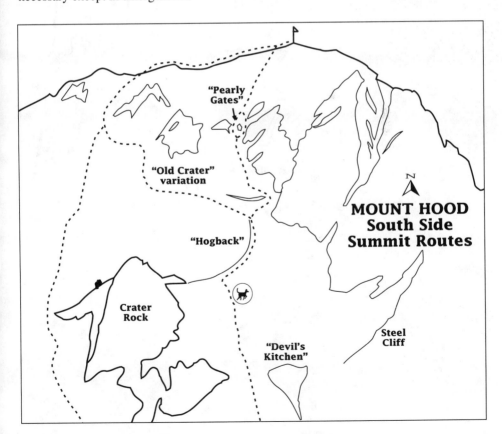

The **Wy'East** route (②; 8-10 hrs) begins as for the South Side route from Timberline Lodge. Wy'east is a native name for Mount Hood. Ascend to about 7,600 feet, then traverse east across the White River Glacier to the bases of two prominent snow gullies. Ascend either gully and continue to the ridge crest via steep firn slopes. The rock spur is passed on the right. Gain the summit ridge by traversing into a steep gully. This route also can be approached from the Mount Hood Meadows ski area. Rockfall hazard.

Cooper Spur Approach

Most of the routes originating from Cooper Spur were climbed by Will and Doug Langille, sons of Sarah Langille, who was hostess of Cloud Cap Inn during its heyday. The Langille brothers frequently guided guests to the summit of Mount Hood around the turn of the century. Cloud Cap Inn, a historic building on Cooper Spur, sits at 6,000 feet on the northeast slope of Mount Hood. The inn is closed to the public, but serves as headquarters for the Crag Rats climbing club (Hood River, Oregon).

To reach the inn and the Cooper Spur trailhead, drive State Highway 35 about 20 miles south from Hood River (or about 18 miles north from the U.S. 26-State Rte. 35 junction) to Polallie Campground. Take Forest Service Road 3512 west to the Cooper Spur ski

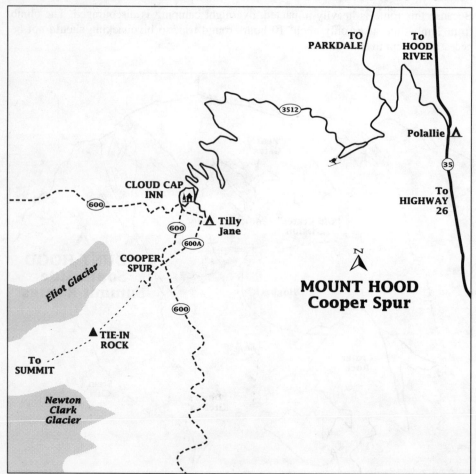

Mount Hood 111

area (well-marked and paved). From the ski area, continue up a curvy, primitive road to its end at the Cloud Cap Inn or Tilly Jane Campground. The Cooper Spur Road is snow-free after July in most years. In winter, there is a marked ski trail leading to the spur from the ski area.

Trails to Cooper Spur and North Face routes begin from road's end (Timberline Trail 600 from Cloud Cap Inn, Spur 600A from Tilly Jane Campground). The north side of Mount Hood is part of Mount Hood Wilderness.

Cooper Spur ★ 4-6 hrs

Cooper Spur is the most straightforward route on Mount Hood. It first was ascended by the Langille brothers in 1897. From Cloud Cap Inn or Tilly Jane Campground, ascend to Tie-in Rock (as for Newton-Clark Glacier Route). Continue straight up steep snow slopes (50° near the top) to the summit.

Cooper Spur. Photo: Austin Post, U. S. Geological Survey

This route has no technical difficulty, but does have avalanche exposure. It is quite steep and exposed, particularly high up. Falls from this route are common and often fatal – this is not to imply that climbers regularly fall and die on this route, but rope teams occasionally have been dragged to their demise during their descent. A few lucky climbers, however, have survived the ride to the Eliot Glacier. Be extra careful during the descent.

Eliot Glacier/Sunshine Route   6-8 hrs

This route was first climbed solo by Will Langille in 1892, and is popularly known as the "Sunshine Route" because it is usually in sunlight all day. It is a fine, non-technical outing that is very popular.

From Cooper Spur, traverse Eliot Glacier and ascend its right slope towards "Horseshoe Rock" (a small rock formation high up), which is most easily passed on the right. A late-season bergschrund often blocks passage beyond Horseshoe Rock; it usually can be skirted on the right. Continue up Cathedral Ridge to the summit.

Elliot Glacier Headwall (④; 6-8 hrs): A more challenging variation climbs through the Eliot Glacier icefalls and ascends the steep headwall. It features mixed rock and/or steep snow and ice (60°, possibly Class 5 rock if not completely iced over), with considerable rockfall hazard unless well-frozen. Before Yocum Ridge was climbed, Eliot Headwall was considered the most difficult route on Mount Hood. Grade II.

Other Routes Reached Via Cooper Spur

The **Newton Clark Glacier** route (②; 8 hrs) is ususally approached from Cooper Spur. From Cooper Spur (below or at "Tie-in Rock"), descend to Newton Clark Glacier and climb directly upward via steep firn slopes on the headwall to the crater rim, finishing via the **Wy'east** gully. Rockfall and avalanche hazard.

The **North Face** (④; 6-8 hrs) has two prominent gullies and three rock ribs that offer straightforward climbing routes. Approach as for Eliot Glacier, staying left to meet the headwall wherever it's easiest to pass the bergschrund. There are five distinct routes reported on the North Face: **Northeast Spur** (Grade II); **East Gully** (Grade III); **East Rib** (Grade III); **West Gully** (Grade III); and **North Cleaver** (Grade III). Rockfall and avalanche hazard exists on all routes. Best when well frozen.

The **Coe Glacier Icefall** route (③; 6-8 hrs) essentially climbs directly through the 1,000-foot icefall of Coe Glacier. Reach the summit via the **Sunshine Route.** Icefall hazard. Grade II. Preview the route from Cloud Cap Inn.

Cathedral Ridge Approach

The approach to Cathedral Ridge begins on Forest Service Road 18 from Zig Zag. The simplest route heads 10 mi north on Lolo Pass Road to Forest Service Road 1828; take a hard right at the pass and drive 3 mi. From here, a very hard left onto Forest Service Road 118 (unpaved) reaches the Top Spur trailhead. Hike Top Spur Trail 758 a quick half-mile to the PCT (which is hiked on briefly), then join Timberline Trail 600 for a 3-mile climb up Bald Mountain Ridge. Just above four quick switchbacks, leave Timberline Trail on a way trail continuing toward Mount Hood. After about .25 mi, you will reach McNeil Shelter, a historic stone hut. Bivouac near the hut, or higher on the ridge.

Mount Hood 113

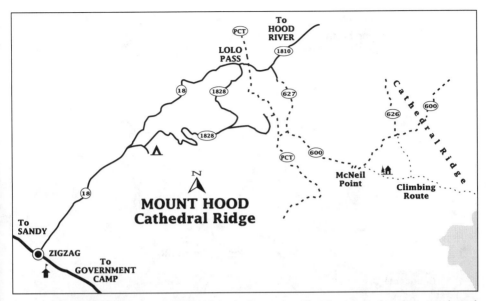

The **Cathedral Ridge** route (③; 8-10 hrs) is not popular due to its long approach and mostly uninteresting climbing. The lower part of the ridge is a scree slog; the upper section is steep snow or scree. Class 3 or Class 4 may be encountered lower on the ridge, if you get off route.

Illumination Saddle Approach

Routes on the west side of Mount Hood are most easily approached from Illumination Saddle, the prominent notch between Castle Crags and Illumination Rock and a popular basecamp for west-side routes (if fecal remains are a valid indicator). From Timberline Lodge, ascend as for the **South Side Route,** and traverse toward the saddle across the Zig Zag Glacier at about 9,000 feet. Crevasses are rarely a problem on Zig Zag Glacier, but they are present. If you start early enough, you can hike up beside the ski lift, then veer northwest from its top more directly to the saddle. Illumination Rock, a crumbly spire, may be climbed by several routes, nearly all of which feature Class 5 climbing on shattered rock ("the best rock on Mount Hood").

Yocum Ridge ⑤ 12+ hrs

"This route is extremely hazardous and is not recommended by the author or anyone else in his right mind." Ross Petrie, 1961. Ditto.

This, the most-technical route on Mount Hood, was first climbed by Fred Beckey and Leo Scheiblehner in 1959. Periods of cold weather, with snow and ice cover, are prerequisites for climbing this route. Climbers attempting this route during any other conditions should expect continuous, copious rockfall and Class 5 climbing on nightmarishly loose rock. Serious commitment, poor rock and high exposure make it a poor choice for any but the most skilled climbers. Nevertheless, like many other "suicide" routes, it remains a popular pseudo-classic objective; a rite of intitiation for serious northwest climbers. Grade V, Class 5.

A gully reaching the saddle above the third gendarme is commonly used to escape the ridge when the upper buttress is unclimbable – and as an alternate start to the upper buttress to avoid the lower ridge. An exit traverse to Sandy Glacier Headwall from the upper snow saddle has been done, but is not recommended any more than the final headwall.

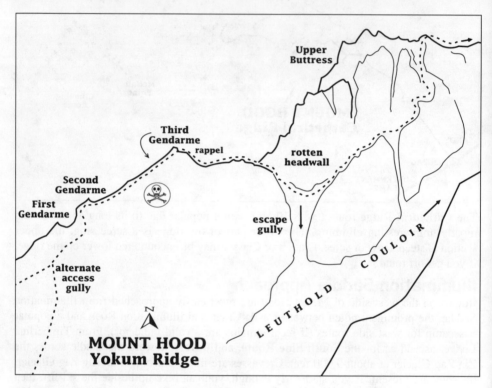

This route has abundant loose rock, extreme rockfall hazard and bad protection. Take pitons and ice screws for luck if nothing else.

Other Routes Approached via Illumination Saddle

To reach the **Sandy Glacier Headwall** route (④; 8-10 hrs) from Illumination Saddle, descend onto Reid Glacier and skirt Yocum Ridge. Ascend Sandy Glacier and its headwall (50° slopes). Rockfall and avalanche hazard. Grade III.

The **Reid Glacier Headwall – Leuthold Couloir** route (②; 6-8 hrs) is an excellent climb when conditions are good; otherwise, it is an avalanche/rockfall funnel. From the saddle, cross the Reid Glacier and ascend the obvious snow chute through the headwall, angling left toward Yocum Ridge. Pass "The Hourglass," a narrow spot in the coulour, and continue to the right at the couloir's end toward the summit. Rockfall and avalanche hazard. Grade II.

Two narrow gullies right of Leuthold Couloir are sometimes climbed under frozen conditions; otherwise, they are rockfall funnels.

To climb the **Castle Crags** route (②; 4-6 hrs), climb exposed scree or snow slopes opposite Illumination Rock. At the upper buttress, traverse right along a scree or snow shelf to the ridge crest. Continue along the ridge crest, bypassing rotten gendarmes, to the summit slopes. Several variations are possible (Class 3 to easy 5); none are recommended. Rocfall hazard. Grade II.

Mount Hood's westside routes. Photo: Austin Post, U. S. Geological Survey

Mount Jefferson, with Jefferson Park and Russell Glaciers, from the northwest.

Photo: Austin Post, U. S. Geological Survey

Chapter Nine:
Mount Jefferson
Oregon, 10,497 ft./3199m

Oregon's second-highest mountain is Mount Jefferson, a striking peak situated between Albany and Bend in north-central Oregon. Like Mount Hood, "Jeff" is a landmark of the Oregon Cascades. Smaller than Mount Hood, and certainly less accessible, Jefferson nevertheless is a popular climb, being a bit more rugged than Hood, and offering a more traditional climbing experience than the typical up-and-down-in-a-day ascent of Mount Hood. Approach hikes are about five miles, and lakeside campsites in Jefferson Park are favorite bases for weekend climbing parties.

Mount Jefferson is an older volcano that has not been notably active in recent geologic history. Glaciers have worn down Jefferson's softer flanks, while the central vent and basaltic dikes and ridges have remained at least partly intact. Its volcanic history is relatively unimportant, except that it has very loose rock and a difficult summit pinnacle that has withstood the ravages of erosion that have worn down its surrounding flanks. After the glaciers are finished with it, Mount Jefferson will become just another rotten Central Oregon volcanic horn, like Mount Washington or Three Fingered Jack.

Although the mountain reportedly was first climbed in 1888, and had been climbed at least three times prior to the turn of the century, it was thought impossible by many climbers as late as 1905. Modern parties find few obstacles to success on the mountain, although the summit pinnacle still repels its share, mostly in disgust or fear. Most of Mount Jefferson's routes involve minimally technical glacier and ridge climbing, usually with Class 3 and maybe a little Class 4 or 5 climbing, but the summit pinnacle requires basic routefinding skills on its short, rotten Class 3, 4 and 5 rock pitches.

MOUNT JEFFERSON

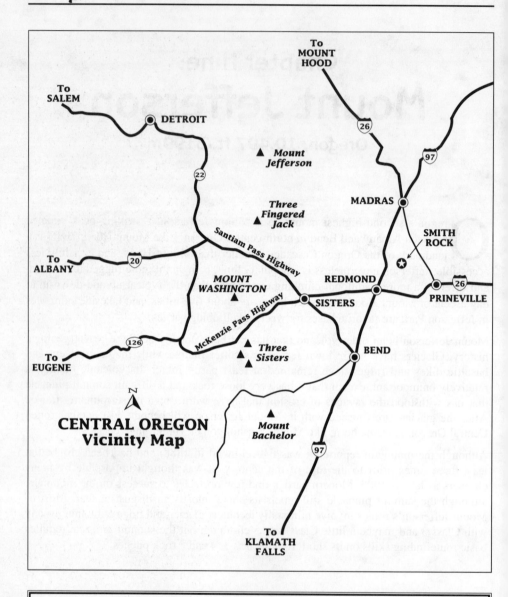

For information about permits and access, contact:

Detroit Ranger District
HC-73, Box 320
Mill City, OR 97360

(503) 854-3366

Rating details appear on pages 4 through 7 of the Introduction.

Mount Jefferson

Jefferson Park, the most popular area of Mount Jefferson Wilderness and the classic basecamp for ascents of the mountain, suffers from overuse. Please bring stoves instead of relying on natural fuel for cooking and heat, and make an effort to minimize your impact in this area. Self-issue permits are now required for day use of Mount Jefferson Wilderness. Overnight permits are not self-issue, and must be obtained from a ranger district office or other outlet. Whitewater Glacier is on Warm Springs Indian Reservation land, but no special permit is needed unless you are going fishing. This could change, so check with Detroit Ranger District prior to your climb. If you want more information on routes up Mount Jefferson, consult Jeff Thomas' *Oregon High* (Keep Climbing Press, 1991).

Summit Pinnacle Routes

From Red Saddle (the point from which most climbers reach the pinnacle), there are several possible routes to the summit. For the most part, these routes consist of Class 3 and 4 climbing. In the words of Bill Soule of Timberline Mountain Guides:

> "They [the summit pinnacle routes] are short enough to make route-finding insignificant. The climbing consists of third or fourth class with bad to non-existent anchors on the worst rock imaginable. Don't get me wrong. Jefferson is a worthwhile climb, but the summit pinnacle is not the reason why."

The standard summit pinnacle route from Red Saddle begins with a dangerous, steep snow traverse from the west side all the way around to the north side, then climbs loose Class 3 or 4 ledges to the summit. There is a direct route on the west side that gains the saddle between the two summit pinnacles, but this is very loose and not recommended. Other more difficult variations have been done (Class 5.0 to 5.7 reported), but these aren't much better. Any way you go, expect plenty of loose rock.

Routes on the east flank of Mount Jefferson finish via a more direct but equally loose Class 5 route on the northeast side of the pinnacle.

Descents from Mount Jefferson are most easily made via Whitewater Glacier, East Face, or Southwest Ridge, depending upon where you parked your car.

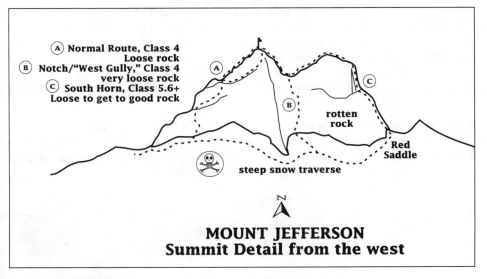

MOUNT JEFFERSON
Summit Detail from the west

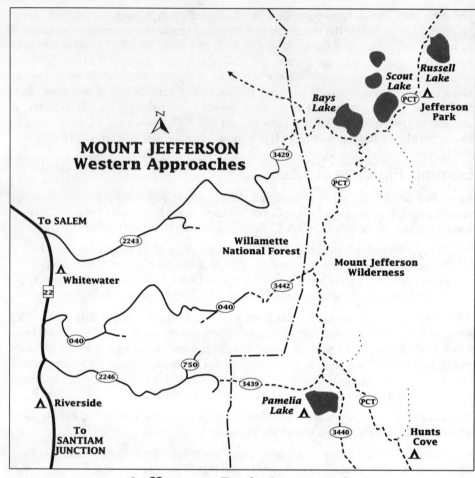

Jefferson Park Approach

The easiest approach to Jefferson Park is via Whitewater Trail. Drive Forest Service Road 2243 from Whitewater Campground (about .5 mi off of State Highway 22, 6 mi east of Idanha). Continue 6 mi past the campground to road's end. Hike Whitewater Trail 3429 along Sentinel Creek 1.5 mi to its junction with Jefferson Park Trail 3373. Head east on Jefferson Park Trail 2.5 mi to the PCT. Continue northeast a short mile to Scout Lake and lovely Jefferson Park.

Camping at Scout and Russell Lakes is popular, but there are many campsites in Jefferson Park that are being rehabilitated due to overuse, and are now closed to camping. Please check with the Forest Service for road and trail conditions and campsite availability when obtaining your permit prior to your climb.

Mount Jefferson 121

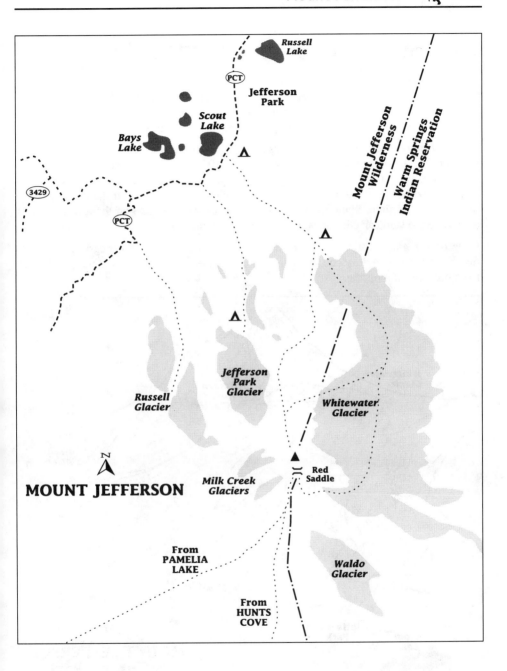

Whitewater Glacier ③ 10-12 hrs

This is the most-frequently climbed route on Jefferson, although it is not the most direct from Jefferson Park. Whitewater Glacier is a broad sheet that will become several distinct smaller glaciers if it melts much more. The glacier is frequently skied to and from the southeast spur, which certainly would save time on the descent.

From Jefferson Park, hike south cross-country to the north flank of the Whitewater Glacier. Routefinding to the glacier can be difficult and time-consuming for the uninitiated. If you have time the night before your ascent, scout the approach to the glacier; it will save you time in the morning. If you camp higher, near the glacier, you'll save even more time. Some parties find themselves short of time on the ascent, so you are advised to start early if you want to reach the summit.

Once on the glacier, traverse south, ascending gradually to the southeast spur. Climb over a short ridge and ascend the spur to Red Saddle (10,000 feet), a stone's fall away from the summit pinnacle.

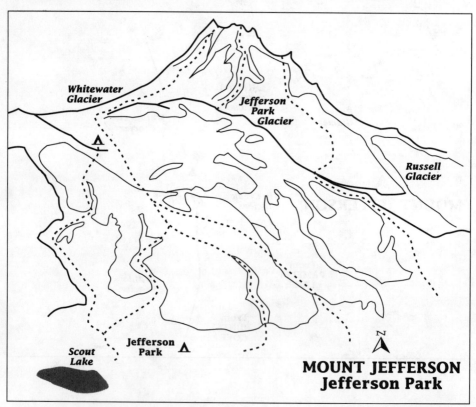

Mount Jefferson   123

A view of Mount Jefferson's Whitewater Glacier.   Photo: Austin Post, U. S. Geological Survey

Jefferson Park Glacier   ★   ③   8-10 hrs

This is the second-most popular route on Mount Jefferson. It is steeper and more alpine in nature than Whitewater Glacier – and more difficult – making it very nearly a worthwhile route (except, of course, for the summit pinnacle).

Ascend from Scout Lake or the PCT/Jefferson Park Trail junction to the east edge of the glacier, and continue more or less directly to the bergschrund. Passing the bergschrund may present a problem; the best choice is to stay right, scrambling up a rock ridge (going left subjects you to more frequent rockfall). A short traverse left above the bergschrund takes you into a shallow cirque that leads to a narrow ridge crest. This ridge has been variously reported as "scrambling" and "Class 5.1," but appears to be on fairly solid rock (by comparison with the summit pinnacle, though not all parties agree). Other variations have been done here, but however you finish, join the North Ridge route to the summit. Grade III.

Other Routes Reached Via Jefferson Park
The following routes are listed counter-clockwise around the mountain.

The **Whitewater Glacier – Warm Springs Couloir** route (④; 8-10 hrs) climbs an obvious couloir up the east face. From the midsection of Whitewater Glacier, ascend the leftmost couloir (steep snow or ice) to the base of the summit pinnacle. Angle right to a snowfield that gives access to the East Arête. Continue up loose rock to the summit. Rockfall and avalanche hazard. Grade III, Class 5.

The dangerous **East Arête** route (④; 8-10 hrs) ascends the prominent narrow rock buttress descending directly from the summit pinnacle. Rockfall hazard. Grade III, Class 5.

Mount Jefferson

Mount Jefferson's Jefferson Park Glacier. Photo: Austin Post, U. S. Geological Survey

The **Whitewater Glacier Headwall** route (④; 8-10 hrs) ascends the face immediately right of the **East Arête,** via many variations. Rockfall and avalanche hazard. Grade II.

The **East Face** route (③; 6-8 hrs) attains the **North Ridge** from the middle of Whitewater Glacier. Continue as for the **North Ridge** route. A variation reportedly climbs through the upper rotten rock buttress (loose Class 4). Rockfall and avalanche hazard.

The **North Ridge** route (③; 6-8 hrs) ascends the north ridge directly from Jefferson Park. The ridge is very straightforward, and also very loose. Approach as for Jefferson Park Glacier, but stay on the crest. Some roped, loose rock pitches may be encountered on the ridge unless snow permits easier climbing. Rockfall hazard. Grade II, Class 3 or 4.

The infrequently-climbed **Russell Glacier** route (③; 10-12 hrs) ascends the Russell Glacier to the Jefferson Park Glacier route at the crux ridge. Rockfall and avalanche danger. Grade III, Class 4 or 5.

The ridge dividing the Jefferson Park and Russell Glaciers reportedly was climbed in either 1906 or 1925.

Pamelia Lake Approach

Pamelia Lake Trail is used to approach several less-appealing westside routes. To reach Pamelia Lake, take Forest Service Road 2246, which leaves State Highway 22 about 7 mi east from Idanha (2 mi north from Riverside Campground). Pamelia Lake Trail 3439 begins just before road's end, leading 2.25 mi to Pamelia Lake and junctions with the PCT and Skyline Trail. Skyline Trail 3440 leads 3 mi south to Hunts Cove.

Both Pamelia Lake and Hunts Cove suffer from overuse, so minimize your impact in these overcrowded areas. Check with Detroit Ranger Station for low-impact camping opportunities. The summit routes reached from these approaches are described counter-clockwise around the mountain.

The **Milk Creek Glacier – North Lobe** route (③; 6-8 hrs) climbs stagnant icefields on the west face of Mount Jefferson. Serious rockfall and avalanche danger. Grade II, Class 4.

The **Milk Creek West Ridge** route (③; 8-10 hrs) follows the prominent scree and lava ridge dividing the lobes of the Milk Creek Glaciers on the west side of Mount Jefferson. Serious rockfall hazard. Grade II, Class 4.

The **Milk Creek Glacier – South Lobe** route (③; 8-10 hrs) ascend the gully south of the ridge, which is the bed for a small, stagnated glacier. Rockfall and avalanche hazard. Grade II, Class 4.

The summit also can be reached via two southwest-slope "dog routes" (③; 10-12 hrs). The **Pamelia Lake** route has been described as "a hot, dry climb," which is "the easiest but most tedious route" on Mount Jefferson. The **Hunts Cove** route is another "long, tedious climb," up the south ridge directly to the southwest shoulder. Rockfall hazard.

Mount Jefferson's west face.

Photo: Austin Post, U. S. Geological Survey

Three Fingered Jack in winter. Photo: Alan Kearney

Chapter Ten:
Three Fingered Jack

Oregon, 7,841 ft./2390m

Three Fingered Jack is among the oldest high volcanoes in the Cascades. The complex internal structure of the now dormant volcano, along with the ravages of erosion by former glaciers, have combined to form the rugged summit of Three Fingered Jack. The mountain is believed to have undergone three distinguishable volcanic building phases, culminating in a basaltic intrusion into a softer andesite cone. Over the epochs, glaciation has worn away the softer material, leaving only the erosion-resistant core. Mount Thielson and nearby Mount Washington share a similar geologic history.

Like Mount Washington, Three Fingered Jack boasts some very poor rock. So lowly-regarded is the rock on Three Fingered Jack that the summit pinnacle is said to vibrate in high winds! The peak was first ascended by the "Boys from Bend" in 1923 (as was Mount Washington). It is not a highly-regarded climb; only the standard route will be described. A full accounting of other routes on Three Fingered Jack, all of which are reportedly very rotten, is contained in Jeff Thomas' *Oregon High*. Just don't say I didn't warn you.

Potable water is scarce here, so bring plenty along. Also, when approaching and descending from the summit, take care not to cause any further erosion or exacerbate what has already been created by heedless herds of climbers. Perhaps the cairn marking the climbers' trail could be removed to truly retain the spirit of the Wilderness Act? Plunge-stepping down anything but snow is not environmentally-sensitive, to say the least.

Fill out a permit prior to entry into Three Fingered Jack Wilderness. Overnight stays require a permit from the Forest Service.

For access information, contact:

Sisters Ranger District P.O. Box 248 Sisters, OR 97759	(503) 549-2111
Detroit Ranger District HC-73, Box 320 Mill City, OR 97360	(503) 854-3366

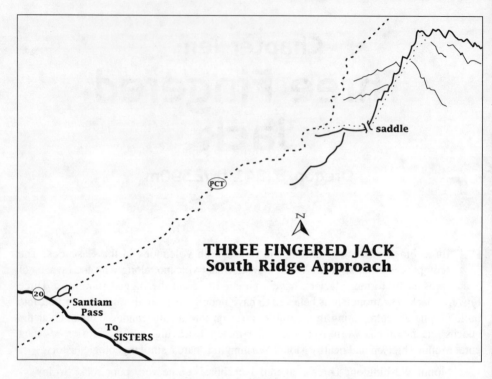

South Ridge ③ 6-8 hrs

The easiest route up Three Fingered Jack begins from Santiam Pass Highway (U.S. 20) via the PCT. The PCT trailhead is a short distance west of Santiam Pass, on a well-marked loop road to the north. After about 5 miles of hiking north, the trail follows the contour around a southern shoulder of Three Fingered Jack (Point 6961 on USGS map), which now comes into full view. Within a half-mile, an obvious climbers' trail leads toward the South Ridge saddle. From the saddle, scramble up the loose ridge. At a point about 200 feet below the summit, a gendarme blocks easy progress. Traverse a narrow, exposed ledge ("The Crawl") on the east side around the gendarme and continue to the summit pinnacle. A concave wall and shallow chimney give relatively solid access to the top.

A rope and a few chocks are recommended for the gendarme traverse and the final pitch to the summit, both of which are very exposed Class 4 or easy Class 5 on less-than-perfect rock. The climbing is easy enough for experienced climbers to manage unroped, but the rock is friable in places, which has contributed to some long falls. This is definitely not a route for inexperienced climbers. A helmet might be useful here, as well as a rope and a few chocks and slings. Grade II, Class 5.0.

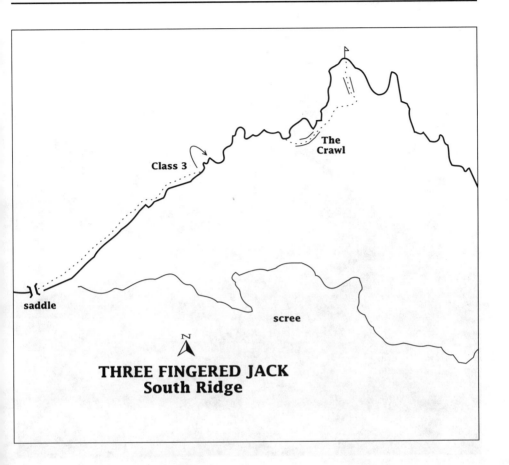

Mount Washington in winter.

Chapter Eleven:
Mount Washington
Oregon, 7,794 ft./2376m

Mount Washington, another rotten remnant of a former volcano, has a well-founded reputation for loose rock. Indeed, within ten years of the mountain's first ascent, the original route had disintegrated. The modern North Ridge route climbs slightly more stable rock closer to the ridge crest.

Mount Washington was first ascended in 1923, one of the last of the peaks in this guide to be climbed. Up until that year, despite numerous attempts, Washington had repelled all comers. All early ascensionists had been unable to pass the first step of the upper North Ridge, which had been chosen as the most-likely route to "go." The "Boys from Bend," perhaps undaunted by the mountain's reputation for hideous looseness and impenetrability, found a passage via a rotten ledge and an even more-rotten chimney. Ervin McNeal boldly led the exposed crux chimney, followed by Leo Harryman, Phil Philbrook, Armin Furrer, Wilbur Watkins and Ron Sellers.

Although Mount Washington has numerous technical rock routes, these will not be included in this guide, partly because few parties will (or will even want to) climb most of these routes, which involve steep, exposed, loose rock. There are said to be some excellent free climbing pitches on Mount Washington, but these are situated between many pitches of ugly rock. Most users of this guide hopefully will prefer to reach the summit by the easiest route possible, rather than grapple with truly bad rock. With the recognition of nearby Smith Rock as one of the world's leading technical rock-climbing areas, fewer ascents of Mount Washington's technical climbs will likely be made. Rock-climbing specialists will undoubtedly prefer a half-mile descent into the Crooked River Gorge than a dry, five-mile ascent of crumbly Mount Washington. However, if you are interested in climbing the technical rock routes on Mount Washington, Jeff Thomas' *Oregon High* (Jeff Thomas, Keep Climbing Press 1991) lists them all. Have fun!

Fill out a permit prior to entering Mount Washington Wilderness. For information contact:

Sisters Ranger District P.O. Box 248 Sisters, OR 97759	(503) 549-2111
Detroit Ranger District HC-73, Box 320 Mill City, OR 97360	(503) 854-3366

Potable water is scarce in Mount Washington Wilderness, so be sure to bring plenty along. Camping within the wilderness is typically hot and dry, and not recommended. Ascents are practical in one day, although some prefer to make an overnight trip, despite limited water supplies and poor camping prospects.

North Ridge ② 6-8 hrs

The north ridge of Mount Washington is approached via the Pacific Crest Trail from near Big Lake. Drive Santiam Pass Highway (U.S. 20) to Hoodoo Ski Bowl. Take Forest Service Road 2690 south, two miles to Big Lake. Just before the lake, turn left onto the old Santiam Wagon Road (Forest Service 500); in a half-mile, you'll reach the junction with the PCT. (Alternatively, social trails south of Big Lake cut from Patjens Lake Trail to the PCT after one mile; it's not much shorter really, and environmentally insensitive to boot.)

Hike south on the PCT about 3.5 miles to a cairn that marks a climbers' path heading east toward the north ridge of Washington. The path follows the contour onto the north ridge (just south of Point 6323), and continues along the east edge of the ridge until a westerly descent around the final pinnacles leads up a loose gully to the prominent saddle.

Most parties rope up at the saddle, as the next 75 feet of climbing to the top of "The Nose" (the first step) is the most difficult on the route. Scramble right 15 feet to a left-leaning chimney. The chimney peters out after 30 feet, where left-angling face climbing reaches another 30 feet the top of the step. This section is Class 4 or easy Class 5. Party-caused rockfall is common on this route. Many parties unrope above The Nose, as the remaining climb is fairly straightforward, featuring unexposed scrambling except for a final short gully. Grade I.

If you feel you need a rope on any section of this route, don't be afraid to tie one on. This is definitely not a route for inexperienced climbers. A helmet might be useful. Rappels may be made down the steepest sections on the descent.

Mount Washington

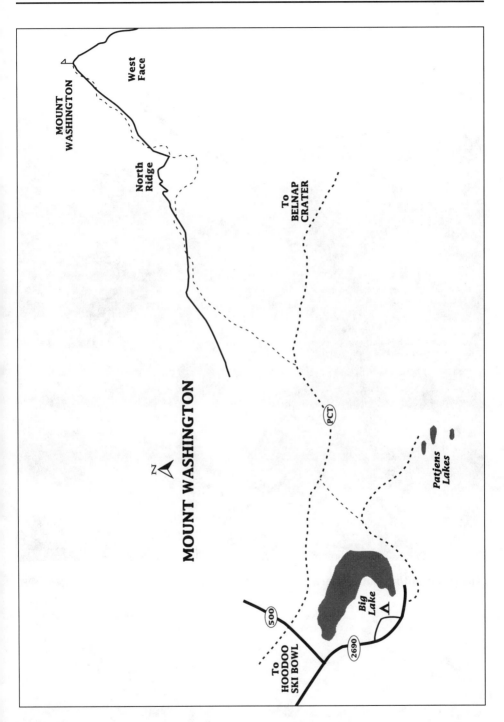

The crater of the South Sister.

Chapter Twelve:
Three Sisters
Oregon

The Sisters are three prominent volcanoes situated just east of Bend, each rising to just over 10,000 feet. The peaks are moderately glaciated, although these glaciers are mild and relatively uncrevassed compared to the glaciers on Mount Shasta and Mount Hood. Each of the three mountains can be climbed via relatively simple north-south ridges, except the summit pinnacle of North Sister, which has some loose rock climbing. It is common for climbers to traverse the entire group in a single long day (a "Three Sisters Marathon"). For those not up to a one-day marathon, it is more feasible to complete the traverse with a bivouac.

The Three Sisters have been named "Faith," "Hope" and "Charity" by some kind, naïve soul; more aptly, they are Big Sister (South), Little Sister (Middle) and Ugly Sister (North). All are included in the expansive Three Sisters Wilderness.

Fill out a permit prior to day-use entry into Three Sisters Wilderness. Overnight stays require a permit from one of the ranger district offices. There are camping and campfire setbacks in certain areas of Three Sisters Wilderness; be sure to check at ranger stations or trailheads for specifics. For more information on routes on any of the Sisters, consult Jeff Thomas' *Oregon High* (Keep Climbing Press, 1991).

For access information, contact:

Sisters Ranger District P.O. Box 248 Sisters, OR 97759	(503) 549-2111
Bend Ranger District 1645 Highway 20 East Bend, OR 97701	(503) 388-5664
McKenzie Ranger District McKenzie Bridge, OR 97413	(503) 822-3381
Oakridge Ranger District Highway 58 Oakridge, OR 97492	(503) 782-2291

136 Three Sisters

Rating details appear on pages 4 through 7 of the Introduction.

An overview of Three Sisters and Broken Top from the southeast.

Photo: Austin Post, U. S. Geological Survey

North Sister
10,085 ft./3074m

North Sister is the oldest and most rugged of the Three Sisters group. The mountain's west flank is fairly moderate, but the east face is characteristically craggy and very unstable. North Sister once rose to an estimated height of over 11,000 feet. However, the mountain's construction was its downfall. The soft andesite cone has been erased, the crater is indistinguishable, and the remaining volcano has lost about one-third of its original mass to erosion. What is left is a big heap of loose volcanic rubble. North Sister, "the Black Beast of the Cascades," is a big, ugly mountain with two distinct pinnacles and numerous crumbly gendarmes decorating its scree-laden ridges. The higher horn is "Prouty" and a sub-summit is "Glisan" (named for venerated members of the Mazamas climbing club).

Because of the variable volcanic composition, all routes involve climbing remarkably unstable rock with high rockfall hazard. Massive rockfalls on the east and west faces are likely in the future; minor rockfalls are nearly constant on North Sister, except when the mountain is coated with ice. Any route in a couloir or gully on North Sister is a veritable shooting range (the main chute up Prouty is called the "bowling alley"). Thus, North Sister is a more serious objective than Middle or South Sisters. Expect loose rock and copious rockfall no matter where you venture on this mountain, even under the best conditions. All things considered, this peak is not particularly safe by any route. You should come when the mountain is frozen and has some snow cover, so some of the loose rocks will be frozen in place during your climb.

Because of rockfall, all routes on the east and west faces of North Sister are extremely dangerous, and none except the easier routes is often climbed. If you must climb North Sister, do so by one of the ridge routes, preferably the South or Southeast Ridges. Helmets should be considered mandatory for all routes on North Sister. Winter conditions may reduce rockfall hazard, but will by no means eliminate it completely.

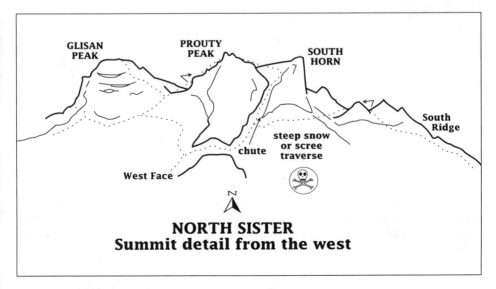

NORTH SISTER
Summit detail from the west

138 Three Sisters

Obsidian Trail Approach

Routes originating from the North-Middle Sister saddle begin from the well-signed Obsidian Trailhead 3528, which begins just off of State Highway 242 southwest of McKenzie Pass. Hike 3.5 mi to a junction. Take the left fork (Spur 3528A) 1 mi to the former site of Sunshine Shelter and a junction with the PCT (now known as "Sunshine Junction" or simply "Sunshine"). From Sunshine junction, hike cross-country 1.5 miles east up your choice of climbers' trails. The trails lead either to the Collier Glacier col, the northwest ridge of North Sister or the Renfrew Glacier.

Three Sisters 139

South Ridge 4-6 hrs

"The conquest of this mountain is probably one of the most brilliant feats ever attempted in America." Photo caption in 1905 *Mazama*.

This route was first ascended in 1910 by H.H. Prouty, the first member of a large Mazama party to surmount the summit pinnacle. It is the most popular route up North Sister, only because it is the most straightforward, but even so it is not very safe.

From the high end of Collier Glacier, traverse north along the rotten ridge to the summit pinnacle, staying left of the several gendarmes along the way. Pass below a prominent rock buttress via a snow or scree traverse ("the most hazardous part of the climb," say some) and ascend a chute (the "bowling alley") to the gap between the Prouty horns. Staying high and right at the top to avoid loose rock, then scramble north to the summit over more stable rock. When there is no snow in the gully, come prepared for loose Class 4. The traverse is best when snow-covered, worse when scree, and treacherous when patchy snow and scree. Grade II, Class 4. Descend the route.

The Collier Glacier descends from the south ridge of the North Sister.

Photo: Austin Post, U. S. Geological Survey

140 Three Sisters

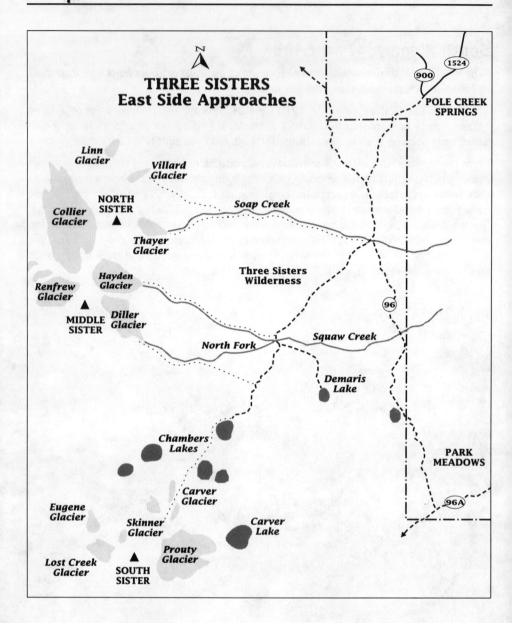

Pole Creek Springs Approach

Routes on the east side of the North and Middle Sisters are approached via Pole Creek Springs. From McKenzie Pass (State Highway 242), head south on the well-marked Pole Creek Springs Road 15 (or if coming from McKenzie Pass, turn south on Forest Service Road 1018 and follow to its junction with Road 15). Follow Road 15 to its end (about 3 mi from the junction).

Pole Creek Springs Trail 96D leads about 1.5 mi to a junction with Three Sisters Trail 96, the main north-south trail east of the Sisters. Cross-country hiking west from this junction, following Soap Creek, approaches the east face of North Sister.

Middle Sister's east face can be reached by hiking cross-country to Hayden Glacier from about halfway along Chambers Lakes Trail 96B, which is about 0.5 mi south of the Pole Creek Springs/Three Sisters trail junction. The northside routes on South Sister also are accessible from Chambers Lakes via Pole Creek Springs Trail.

Erosion on climbers' trails is heavy, and lakeside campsites are overused, so make an effort to minimize your impact. Permits are required for overnight visits. The following North Sister summit routes can be reached via Pole Creek Springs.

The **Southeast Ridge** (3; 6-8 hrs) is reached by hiking two miles on Chambers Lakes Trail 96B, then heading northwest cross-country to the ridge. Rockfall hazard. Grade II.

The **Thayer Glacier Headwall** route (3; 6-8 hrs) is reported in *Oregon High*. It appears very dangerous, with rockfall and avalanche hazard. Grade III.

The **East Arête** route (4; 6-8 hrs) is reached via Thayer Glacier. Ascend the glacier and the prominent rib left of the main east-face couloir. Join the couloir route at the top, and skirt right around Glisan to the saddle. Rockfall hazard. Grade III.

The **East Face – Early Morning Couloir** route (3; 6-8 hrs) climbs the obvious east-face couloir. A rockfall funnel; some avalanche danger. Grade III.

The **East Face – Villard Glacier** route (3; 6-8 hrs) ascends the glacier over the shoulder of Glisan to the **Northwest Ridge.** Rockfall and avalanche hazard. Grade III.

The **Northeast Arête** route (3; 6-8 hrs) is reached by traversing the Collier Glacier and the north ridge to the cleaver dividing the Linn and Villard Glaciers. Ascend the cleaver to the north ridge. Rockfall hazard. Grade III.

The **Linn Glacier Headwall** route (4; 8-10 hrs) ascends the glacier through its headwall via a central snow chute (rockfall funnel) to the north ridge. Rockfall/avalanche hazard. Grade III.

The following two routes are approached via the Obsidian Trail:

The **Northwest Ridge** route (③; 8-10 hrs) is reached by traversing the Collier Glacier or moraines, skirting south of Little Brother, to the northwest ridge. Where the ridge becomes too narrow, drop down on the west side. A loose traverse around Glisan leads to the saddle dividing Glisan from Prouty. Said to be the "safest" route up North Sister. Rockfall hazard. Grade II, Class 4 (on Prouty).

A few routes climb the crumbly **West Face** (③; 4-6 hrs; rockfall). They ascend from the Collier Glacier more or less directly to the "bowling alley" chute. Not for large parties. Grade II, Class 4.

Middle Sister
10,047 ft./3062m

Middle Sister is a simple cone that has suffered some east-face erosion. It is fairly unremarkable, with a few challenging routes on the east face. Routes on this face have extreme rockfall danger, and should be climbed only when well frozen. See the East Side Approach map in the North Sister section for approach

North Ridge ⓪ 4-6 hrs

information.
Approach as for the North Sister's South Ridge, or more directly via Renfrew Glacier. From the col dividing North and Middle Sister, ascend the easy snow-and-cinder ridge to

South Side ⓪ 4-6 hrs

the summit. One hour from the saddle.
There are numerous possible routes that climb the south slope and southeast ridge via snow or scree. None involve technical climbing.

Other Middle Sister Summit Routes

Approach the **Diller Glacier Headwall** route (④; 5-7 hrs) from the east via Pole Creek Springs, or cross over the col and drop down across the Hayden Glacier to the Diller Glacier. Ascend the steep snow chute on the left side of the rotten face. A 90-foot rightward traverse reaches the final snow slopes to the summit. Grade III. Rockfall and avalanche hazard.

The **East Face** route (④; 5-7 hrs) is approached via Chambers Lake Trail and Soap Creek Ridge to Hayden Glacier (or drop over the col from the west). Ascend the glacier to the base of the east face. Angle left near the snow chute on Diller Glacier route, then cut right above the bergschrund up a steep gully. Pass a short rock band above and continue to the summit. Grade III. Rockfall and avalanche hazard.

Three Sisters   143

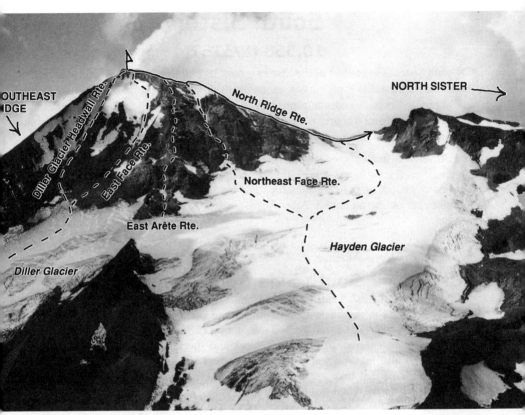

Middle Sister and Hayden Glacier from the east.   Photo: Austin Post, U. S. Geological Survey

The **East Arête** route (④; 6-8 hrs) is a fairly technical climb up the arête dividing the Diller and Hayden Glacier headwalls. Cross the glaciers to the base of the arête. Climb steepening snow and pass a pinnacle on the right to the base of a rock band. Pass the band just left of a wide couloir, climbing just more than one rope-length of Class 4 rock. Continue another rope length of steep snow to a second rock band; pass this via a Class 5.6 chimney right of the arête. Traverse right and go up to the crest of the arête. Continue up snow to where the arête meets the North Ridge. Grade III. Rockfall and avalanche hazard.

The **Northeast Face** route (④; 6-8 hrs), the most technical on Middle Sister, ascends an obvious couloir and gullies directly above the Hayden Glacier, angling left near the top to the North Ridge. This is an active rockfall funnel, so beware! Grade III, Class 5.6. Rockfall and avalanche hazard.

South Sister
10,358 ft./3157m

South Sister is the tallest of the Sisters group. Its eruptive history is similar to that of most of the other Oregon volcanoes. Built atop a basaltic base, the mountain is composed of soft andesite topped by a harder basaltic cone. The mountain has a symmetrical form, and a nearly perfectly-preserved summit crater. More recent eruptions have been from basal or lateral vents, which have produced dacite and obsidian flows.

Most of South Sister's routes have little or no technical challenge, although a few pass through difficult rock bands. There are abundant stone windbreaks along the crater rim, providing breathtaking bivouac sites for those possessed with the insane desire to carry overnight gear up the mountain. After August, a small lake (Oregon's highest) forms in the crater.

South Sister vies with Mount St. Helens for the title of the most-climbed glaciated volcanic peak in North America.

South Side Approaches

South Sister Climbers' Trail (4-6hrs): South Sister Climbers' Trail 36 begins from Devil's Lake, and is the easiest, most-direct and most-frequently-used route to the summit of South Sister. The trail goes to the summit (5.75 mi one way), providing snow-free access for adventurers of all shapes, sizes and species on summer weekends after July. This trail also may be reached from Moraine Lake via Green Lakes Trail. It is a long, tedious, crowded hike – great if you're a hiker, lousy if you're a climber. The views are worth the hike, but just barely.

Green Lakes Trail: Green Lakes Trail is the common approach for most routes on South Sister's south and east sides. The trail begins from a well-signed trailhead just west of Soda Creek Campground (on Highway 46 west of Bend, at Sparks Lake), and leads 4.5 miles to Green Lakes. There are two trails, Forest Service Trail 11 and the more-scenic Trail 11A, that reach Moraine Lake Trail 17. Some parties camp at or near Green Lakes and make a round-trip ascent the next morning. No campfires are permitted within .5 mi of Green Lakes, and campsites must be more than 100 feet away from lake shores. This is a highly-impacted area, so take care.

South Ridge – Green Lakes 4-6 hrs

From Green Lakes, ascend directly to the head of the southeastern drainage basin that leads to the south ridge/slope. Don't climb the gully directly, but find a "trail" on the right (stay right, nearer the trees, to avoid unnecessary erosion of this heavily-damaged slope). Continue up a steep climbers' trail and snow slopes, then skirt around Lewis Glacier to the South Sister Climbers' Trail. The final 1 mi to the summit follows "the Mother of all cinder ridges." Bring plenty of water and don't be ashamed to take a rest break; everyone else does.

The Lewis Glacier offers a direct variation, but won't save much time on the ascent. It also offers an appealing glissading shortcut on the way down, but is steep and has hidden crevasses. Try not to dislodge too much pumice on the way down, as rolling rock could

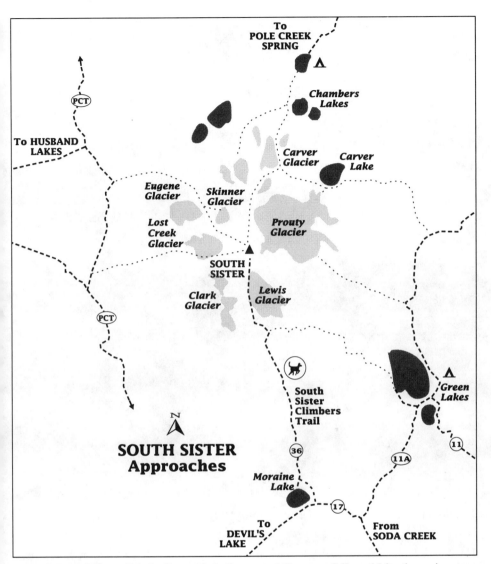

cause injury. This trail is badly eroded. Step carefully, as a fall could land you in some very rough scree.

Other South Sister Summit Routes
Routes are described counter-clockwise around the mountain from the South Ridge route.

The **East Ridge – Old Crater** route (①; 4-6 hrs) climbs from Green Lakes. Ascend the gentle east ridge to the summit, staying left of the crest as necessary. The final portion of the ridge is the rim of one of South Sister's craters. A very tedious climb.

The **Prouty Glacier** route (②; 6-8 hrs) climbs the largest glacier on South Sister. From the northernmost point of Green Lakes, hike cross-country up an obvious, low-angled gully to the glacier's south flank. Ascend the glacier, passing the headwall via a snow chute and rock. Rockfall hazard.

The South Sister's Lewis Glacier and South Ridge – Green Lakes route.
Photo: Austin Post, U. S. Geological Survey

The **North Ridge** route (②; 4-6 hrs) usually is climbed only because it's the fastest way to the summit of South Sister if you want to complete a Three Sisters Marathon. From Green Lakes, follow the contour past Prouty Glacier to the obvious ridge. Ascend a long cinder slope more than halfway to the summit until you're halted by a red-rock buttress. A short, loose traverse leads to the right flank of the buttress, where an easy snow or cinder slope leads to the crater rim just below the summit. Rockfall hazard. Grade II, Class 3 or 4.

The **Silver Couloir** route (④; 8-10 hrs) ascends the leftmost north face couloir. From the head of Skinner Glacier, ascend the couloir directly. Rockfall and avalanche hazard. Attempt only when well frozen. Grade III, Class 4.

The **North Face Couloir** route (④, 8-10 hrs) is the prominent right-side couloir on the north face. It is a bit more difficult than Silver Couloir. Rockfall and avalanche hazard. Attempt only when well frozen. Grade III, possibly 5.6 A3 and/or steep ice.

Routes on the South Sister's **West Side** (◎; 4-6 hrs) can be approached from the Pacific Crest Trail via Hinton, Separation or Mesa Creeks. Several possible routes exist, climbing intervening ridges that divide Eugene Glacier, Lost Creek Glacier and Clark Glacier. None is technically difficult unless you really try to make it hard. There is frequent rockfall from the glacier headwalls. These are best when snow-covered; otherwise, they are just boring cinder slogs – like the South Ridge, but without a trail.

Prouty Glacier and Carver Lake on South Sister. Photo: Austin Post, U. S. Geological Survey

Broken Top's Bend Glacier; Mount Bachelor in the background.

Photo: Austin Post, U. S. Geological Survey

Chapter Thirteen:
Broken Top
Oregon, 9,175 ft./2797m

Broken Top is a craggy volcanic remnant that hosts two glaciers situated at the eastern border of the Three Sisters Wilderness, directly north of Mount Bachelor. Broken Top has had a violent eruptive history, including a massive hot avalanche that devestated an estimated 200-square-mile area, including what are now suburbs of Bend. The mountain was significantly higher at one time, but the combination of being blown up and worn down by glaciation took a lot off the top. Interestingly, climbers can see the former interior of the volcano, including its stratification, which has been revealed by erosion.

The routes all involve rock of varying degrees of difficulty, inconsistency and instability. Rockfall is a real danger on all Broken Top routes, and helmets should be considered mandatory. Like North Sister, no route on Broken Top is really recommended. If all you want to do is summit, take the Northwest Ridge route. The Northwest Ridge is the fastest and safest descent for all routes on Broken Top. Some glacier travel is required for all routes except the Northwest Ridge.

Refer to **Chapter Twelve: Three Sisters** for approach and permit information. For more route detail, see Jeff Thomas' *Oregon High* (Keep Climbing Press, 1991).

Rating details appear on pages 4 through 7 of the Introduction.

150 Broken Top

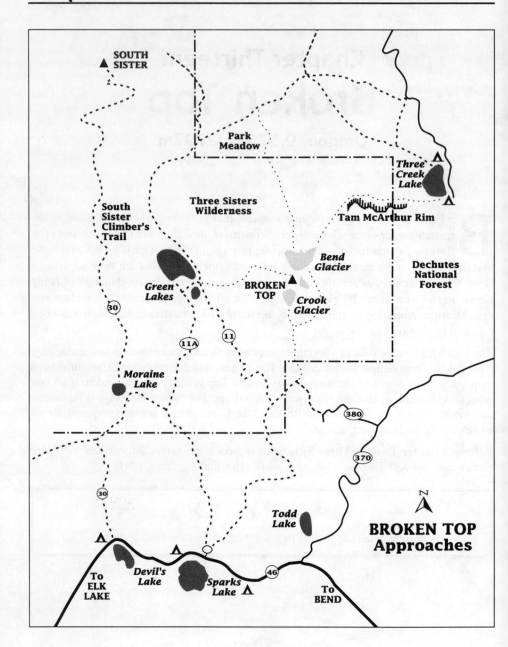

Northwest Ridge 4-6 hrs

From Green Lakes Trail Junction, hike cross-country to the east and ascend to an obvious saddle on the Northwest Ridge. Tedious scree slopes lead directly up the ridge to a point just below where it abuts the summit block. Pass a very short rock band (loose Class 4) to the base of the summit block. A rightward ledge traverse leads to a very loose but easy scramble to the summit. This route is the most direct and easiest way to the summit of Broken Top and back down, and is thus the most popular. Grade II, Class 4 or easy 5.

When snow-covered, it is possible to climb the western (scree) slopes more or less directly to the upper ledge. However, these slopes are avalanche-prone and in the path of rockfall.

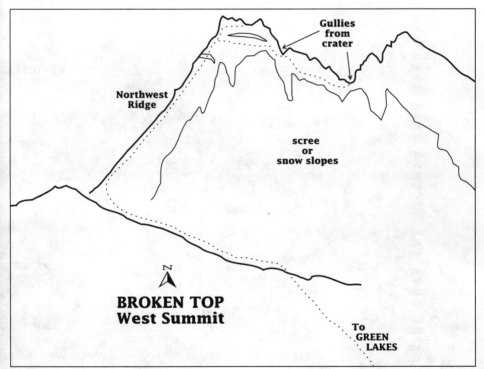

Crook Glacier – Crater Wall 4-6 hrs

Approach via the rough but scenic Todd Lake Road 370 (about 2 mi east of the Bachelor Butte turnoff). There are some monster potholes along the way, so watch out! At about 4 mi, take a left turn on Road 380 (not on Road 378, which ends in a loop much farther south of Broken Top). From road's end, Crater Gulch Trail 10 leads about 0.5 mi to Crater Creek. Follow the creek north (cross-country) to Crook Glacier.

Cross the glacier toward the west crater wall. Ascend the leftmost of two obvious gullies in the crater's west wall. Don't try to climb the rotten ridge crest; stay west of the crater rim on scree or snow slopes, traversing to join the Northwest Ridge for the final ledge traverse. A variation climbs a higher gully out of the crater; this is steeper but more direct. Another reported route ascends the South Face directly from the crater, via a snow finger and very loose rock.

It is unfortunate that the best routes to the summit of Broken Top are plagued by very loose rock and high exposure to rockfall, particularly after snow has melted away. The gullies should not be climbed or descended unless there is a very heavy snowpack and they are well-frozen. Descend via the Northwest Ridge and hike back to the trailhead via Green Lakes.

A view of Broken Top's crater and Crook Glacier routes.

Photo: Austin Post, U. S. Geological Survey

Other Broken Top Routes
These routes are described counter-clockwise around the mountain from the Crook Glacier route.

The **Northeast Spur** route (③; 5-7 hrs) is approached from Todd Lake Road as for the Crook Glacier, or cross-country from Three Creeks Lake and Tam McArthur Rim (longer). From Road 380, traverse around the southeast flank of Broken Top to a small moraine lake on the east side, then onto southern lobe of the Bend Glacier. Ascend a crumbly spur ridge to the jagged ridge crest and follow this to the summit. Rockfall hazard. Grade II, Class 4.

The **North Face** route (④; 5-7 hrs) climbs a broken heap of mud and shattered rock. The best approach is via Todd Lake Road, as for the Northeast Spur. Traverse around the spur to the Bend Glacier. A snow finger on the right side of the rotten headwall gives access to the route. The gully narrows; above, a rightward traverse on "mud" leads to dangerous climbing on loose rock to the ridge crest. A loose traverse along the crest reaches summit block. Rockfall hazard. Grade II, Class 5 mud.

The frightening **North Face Couloir** route (④; 6-8 hrs) ascends the slanting couloir on the north face. Approach via Todd Lake Road or Park Meadow. Where the North Face route continues above the glacier, a rightward traverse along a scree shelf gives access to the couloir. Continue up the couloir to the north shoulder, dodging rockfall as necessary and join the Northwest Ridge route for the final traverse to the summit. Basically a death route. Grade III, Class 5 mud, rockfall galore.

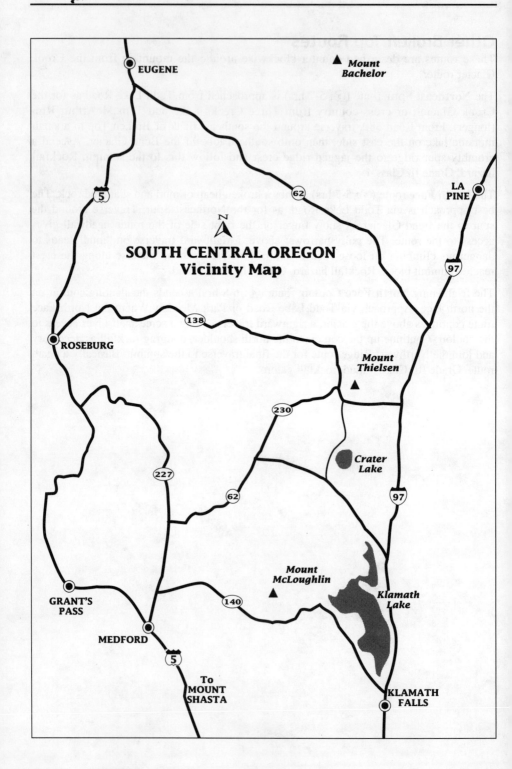

Chapter Fourteen:
Mount Bachelor
9,065 ft./2763m

Mount Bachelor, erstwhile Bachelor Butte, is a high, uniform cone immediately west of Bend on State Highway 46. Bachelor is best known for its skiing, and hosts perhaps the most popular ski area in central Oregon. Geologists have speculated that the volcano is between eruptive cycles. Bachelor has a glacial remnant on its north slope, but north-slope fumaroles, which reportedly sometimes melt snow and trap unwary skiers, give a clue that the mountain is still active.

A 4 mi trail leaves Bachelor Ski Area Road 150 (just off the highway and across from Dutchman's Flat signs); the trail is unmarked, and although it shows up on some maps, you may have trouble finding it due to recent road improvements. It is also possible to ascend directly from the ski area parking lot, although this is not advisable during ski season. To make it more interesting, climb the steep glacier remnant directly.

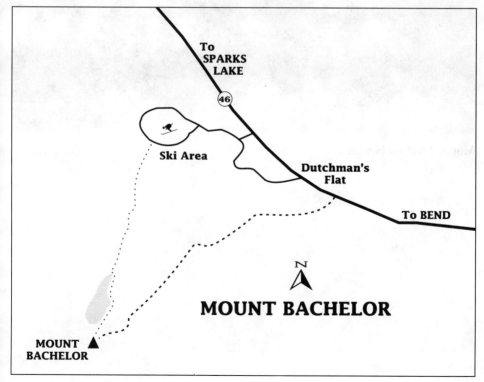

Mount Thielsen in winter.

Photo: Alan Kearney

Chapter Fifteen:
Mount Thielsen
9,182 ft./2799m

"It gives one almost the same feeling as if one were perched high on a swaying tree; it seems as if the steep rock might suddenly collapse in a puff of wind." Jamieson Parker, describing the summit of Mount Thielsen in 1921.

Mount Thielsen is known as "The Lightning Rod of the Cascades" because its summit horn stands so high and is struck by lightning seemingly more often than the summit of any other Cascade peak. Reasons for this are speculative, but there is ample evidence of lightning strikes on the summit area. The fulgurites (lightning-caused deposits) found on the summit are of interest to rock collectors and geologists. Like Mount Washington, Thielsen's summit horn is a remnant of basaltic intrusions in the later stages of the volcano's growth. This erosion-resistant plug intruded on softer material, which has eroded away.

As a climb, Thielsen's standard route is not so difficult that it discourages non-climbers, though it is difficult enough that maybe it should. The only unusual hazard here is that, during stormy weather, the summit is almost certain to be struck by lightning. If a thunderstorm rolls in, descend immediately if you know what's good for you.

As with Mount Washington and Three Fingered Jack, there are other more technical route possibilities on Mount Thielsen (only one done so far, though), but most will be content with reaching this impressive summit by the easy route. Those who are not should consult Jeff Thomas' *Oregon High* (Keep Climbing Press, 1991) for a blow-by-blow account of the **McLaughlin Memorial** route (III, 5.7) up the north face.

To report an accident or other emergency, dial 911 or call Crater Lake National Park, (503) 594-2211.

Mount Thielsen

West Ridge 4-6 hrs

Approach from Diamond Lake parking area, where Mount Thielsen Trail 1456 leads 3 mi east to the PCT. Cross the PCT and hike cross-country up the West Ridge to the base of the summit horn. The upper west ridge features some scrambling; stay near the ridge crest, as it is easier than slogging up the scree slopes. An alternate route drops over the south ridge and slogs up the eastside scree slopes to the base of the summit horn. You also can scramble up the pinnacle-infested south ridge itself. From the southeast base of the horn, one pitch of exposed, fairly solid rock (Class 3 or 4) reaches the summit. Small parties are recommended, since there isn't much room on the summit. Grade I. Though many climbers make this ascent without a rope or protection, you might want a rope and a few chocks in case you change your mind about the final pitch.

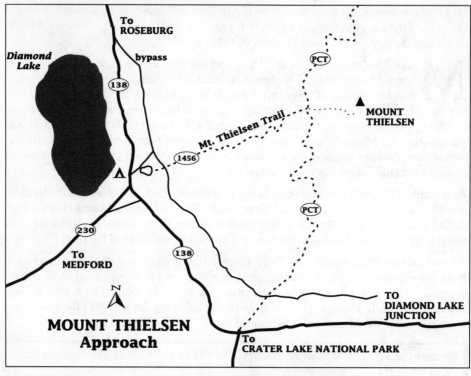

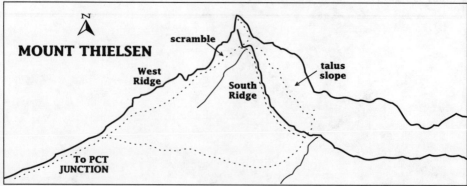

Chapter Sixteen:
Mount McLoughlin
9,495 ft./2894m

Mount McLoughlin is a relatively unknown volcano. Although it is the highest peak between Mount Shasta and South Sister and the sixth-highest peak in Oregon, its unassuming presence is largely ignored by climbers. Like Mount Bachelor, a trail leads to the summit. The climb is relatively easy, and summit views are wide.

Mount McLoughlin is similar to other Cascade volcanoes in at least one respect – its eruptive history. Like nearby Mount Thielsen, it underwent numerous stages of building. However, unlike Thielsen, its summit has been much-less dramatically eroded, leaving a less-rugged profile that is relatively uninspiring compared with Oregon's other high volcanoes.

Mount McLoughlin Trail   3-5 hrs

To reach the trail, drive 3 mi east from Lake of the Woods (33 mi east from Klamath Falls on State Highway 140) to Four Mile Lake Road 350, which leads 2.5 mi north to Mt. McLoughlin Trail 3716. The trail crosses the PCT and climbs strenuously to timberline, from where the path becomes less distinct and much steeper. The entire trip to the summit is about 6 mi one way. Routefinding is easy except during poor weather.

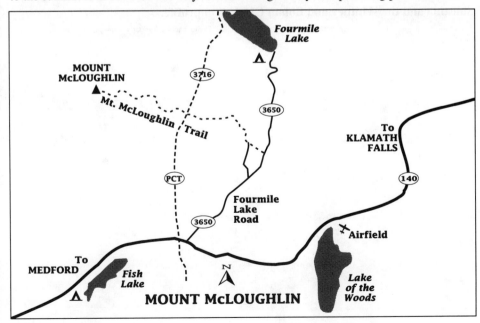

Shastina and the Whitney and Bolam Glaciers in profile.

Photo: Michael Zanger, courtesy Shasta Mountain Guides.

Chapter Seventeen:
Mount Shasta
California, 14,162 ft./4317m

Mount Shasta is the second highest of the Cascade volcanoes, and is the centerpiece of a recently-established wilderness area. Like its relatives farther north, Shasta was formed by various eruptions over the last half million years or so. Intermittent eruptions have built up the main peak, and a lateral vent eruption around the time of the last ice age (or possibly more recently) resulted in present-day Shastina, a parasitic cone. More recent activity has built the summit to its present height, and hot springs just below the summit serve as fair warning that the mountain is merely napping. Mount Shasta appears to be a youthful volcano, as it is relatively unscoured by glaciers and lacks many of the erosion features that are commonplace on volcanoes farther north.

Although it rises more than 10,000 feet above its base – the largest base-to-peak rise of any mountain included in this guide – Mount Shasta is a "gentle giant" compared with some of the northern volcanoes, such as Mount Baker and Mount Rainier. Shasta's glaciers typically are not heavily crevassed until late season, its slopes are not too steep nor very seriously eroded, and few routes to its summit involve truly technical rock or ice climbing. However, this does not mean that Shasta's routes are not serious undertakings. Weather and season often determine difficulty. Mount Shasta's weather is similar to that of Mount Rainier, although it receives much less annual rainfall and snow accumulation. Voluminous lenticular clouds frequently cap the mountain, foretelling the coming of storms. High winds and heavy snows are not uncommon, even when not expected or likely. Like Rainier, Shasta sometimes creates its own weather. When lenticular clouds begin to settle over the summit, a storm is likely brewing, and a hasty descent none too cautious.

Shasta has seven named glaciers, which have been in retreat for many years. The present ice volume of all Mount Shasta glaciers is close to that of the Emmons and Winthrop Glaciers on Mount Rainier. The Whitney Glacier, a narrow ice river two miles long, is California's largest. Mount Shasta's glaciers are active on the northern side of the mountain. Avalanche Gulch and Cascade Gulch once were occupied by Pleistocene glaciers.

Native tribes considered Mount Shasta the center of their universe and an inspiring summer hunting ground. When it spewed smoke, however, they ran, afraid for their lives. A possible sighting of Mount Shasta was recorded in 1817 by Fray Narciso Duran, a Spanish explorer who named what he saw "Jesus Maria." The 1841 Wilkes expedition named the mountain "Shasty Peak." Captain John Fremont called it "Shastl."

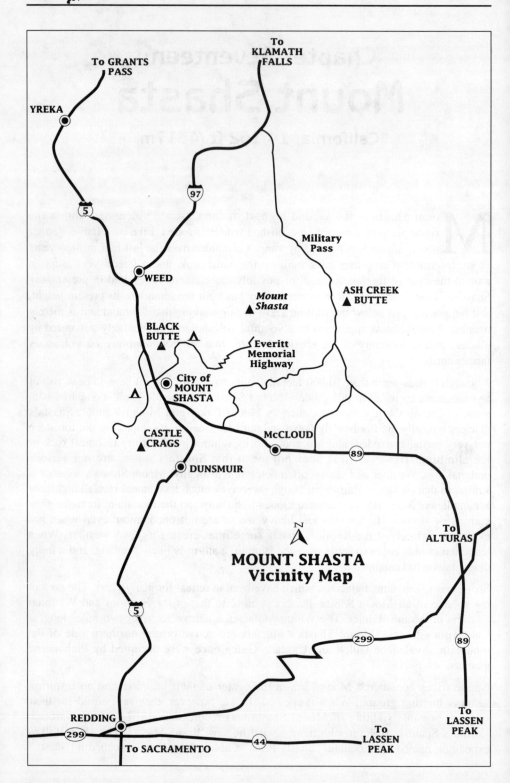

Mount Shasta

The origin of the name has not been pinpointed. "Tshastal" (Russian for "pure" or "white") has been suggested, although "chaste" (French for "pure") or an obscure Indian word are other possible sources. "Shasta" also was believed to be the name of an Indian tribe living near Yreka.

The first recorded ascent of Mount Shasta was by Captain E.D. Pearce, a Yreka sawmill foreman, in 1854. Clarence King climbed the mountain a few years later, spending a night in Shastina's crater. John Muir also climbed the mountain and wrote eloquently of it. Like other Cascade volcanoes, Mount Shasta is a magnet for hikers, climbers and skiers. Many come to Shasta to commune with nature in the presence of this wonderous mountain, and a few religious sects worship Shasta as a "magic mountain." There are astonishing legends of tunnel networks and great telekinetic races living within the mountain. As at Mount Rainier, UFO sightings are regularly reported. Natives still consider Mount Shasta a sacred place. Local devotees, fanatics and kooks also worship Mount Shasta in varying degrees.

Climbers familiar with Mount Shasta should not assume that northern volcanoes are similar climbing objectives. Although similar in size to Mount Rainier (bigger actually), Shasta is more comparable to Mount Hood in climbing terms, in that only a few routes are technically difficult or greatly committing. Each certainly has its difficult routes, but most are, overall, fairly pedestrian (i.e., climbers of all abilities can and do make routine ascents without incident). Generally, the easier routes up Mount Rainier are about as committing as the more difficult routes up Mount Shasta. This is obviously a slightly biased and generalized statement, since there are routes on Shasta that involve serious and technical climbing. However, the differences in latitude, topography, climate and ice volume between the two giants should be evident to even the least experienced observer. This is not to minimize the seriousness or committment of Mount Shasta. Ascents of Shasta are strenuous and can be serious, especially if weather or other conditions conspire against you. Climbing any mountain has its rigors and dangers. Mount Shasta, rising to more than 14,000 feet, has more than most.

Approaches to many of the routes begin on trails or abandoned roads (closed with the formation of the wilderness area), but the trails eventually peter out and cross-country hiking leads to the glaciers and summit. The network of logging roads surrounding Mount Shasta Wilderness is quite complex and confusing; driving to trailheads is a troubling aspect of routefinding for visitors. The lower slopes of Mount Shasta are fairly open, making the approach hikes straightforward – a stark contrast to the dense forests of the northern volcanoes. However, the Mount Shasta landscape is much more fragile than the evergreen forests surrounding, say, Mount Baker. Take care not to do too much damage when not following established trails.

The Mount Shasta Wilderness Plan became effective during the summer of 1990. The plan focuses on finding a balance between recreational use and preservation of the wilderness area. Climbing is recognized as the main recreational attraction of the Mount Shasta Wilderness, and it is doubtful that climbing will be restricted except where necessary to preserve the visual and environmental integrity of the mountain and its surroundings (perhaps Avalanche Gulch). The Forest Service hopefully will improve roads to make approaches easier, and spread climbers out and away from the heavily-used Avalanche Gulch route.

Mount Shasta

The town of Mount Shasta is 60 miles north of Redding on Interstate 5, and is the hub of all non-climbing activity in the area. Everitt Memorial Highway heads north from town toward the mountain. Other approach routes will be discussed within the text. Mount Shasta has all services and accommodations, making a pancake breakfast at Jerry's almost feasible prior to your ascent.

Under the Mount Shasta Wilderness Plan, mandatory registration was proposed for all climbing parties. However, as of January 1991, this system has not been implemented. The proposed system was to issue 75% of permits on a reservation basis, and 25% on a first-come, first-served basis, with party-size limitations for the Avalanche Gulch route.

For information on permit requirements and party size restrictions, contact:

Mount Shasta Ranger District (916) 926-4511
204 West Alma Street
Mt. Shasta, CA 96067

Climbing information and equipment can be obtained from The Fifth Season, the local climbing shop, at 426 North Mt. Shasta Blvd., Mount Shasta, CA 96067 (916) 926-3606. The Fifth Season also has a 24-hour weather and climbing condition hotline, (916) 926-5555. Equipment rentals are available from The Fifth Season. The *Mount Shasta Climber's Review* (copyright The Fifth Season) is a poster-size guide to climbing and skiing on Mount Shasta. *The Mt. Shasta Book* (Wilderness Press, copyright 1989) is a concise guide to all recreational activities within Mt. Shasta Wilderness Area, including hiking, climbing and skiing. The author gratefully acknowledges the acquiescense of Wilderness Press and The Fifth Season, and the contributions of Michael Zanger and Leif Voeltz, in preparing this chapter.

Rating details appear on pages 4 through 7 of the Introduction.

Upper Red Banks. Photo: Michael Zanger, courtesy Shasta Mountain Guides

Mount Shasta

Sierra Club Lodge Approach

Most climbs of Mount Shasta begin from the Sierra Club Alpine Lodge. The simplest approach to the lodge is from Bunny Flat via Everitt Memorial Highway, where a trail leads about 2 mi northwest to the Sierra Club Alpine Lodge and Horse Camp, a heavily-used campsite. Alternatively, many parties approach from Sand Flat; this approach is not recommended during early season unless you are skiing in. New quotas may soon limit camping at or near the lodge, as well as higher on Mount Shasta.

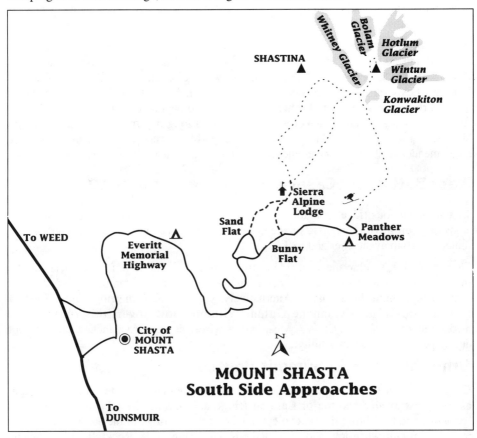

Avalanche Gulch ⓞ 8-10 hrs

This straightforward and simple route was that taken by the first-ascent party, and remains the route of choice for a majority of Shasta's climbers.

Approach as for Cascade Gulch to the Sierra Club Alpine Lodge ("Horse Camp"). Camp here or continue to Lake Helen. "Olberman's Causeway," a stone pathway, leads toward the route from the lodge. This is a heavily-used and very much-abused route. Many parties camp at Lake Helen (10,440 feet). Although there are more than 50 campsites at Lake Helen, the area is overused. Sanitation also is a major problem. The Forest Service has considered setting limits to lessen these impacts.

From Lake Helen, ascend snow slopes (scree in late season) closely right of Casaval Ridge, eventually following the contour right toward "Thumb Rock" saddle and skirting beneath the obvious Red Banks (see photo). Continue upward from the saddle to "Misery Hill," a final steep slope. Traverse the summit col and circle around to the northeast side for a short summit scramble.

There are several possible variations of this route. The "Red Banks" route is the most popular – in fact, more parties take this variation than the route described above. Climb one of the broad chimneys through the Red Banks (best when snow-filled). Crampons may be necessary, as the chimneys are often icy. Rockfall also is possible in the chimneys.

Because of the relative straightforwardness of this route, it is attempted by many ill-prepared and inexperienced climbers. The route should not be taken lightly, however. Beware of avalanches and rockfall, especially while crossing Avalanche Gulch toward Thumb Rock saddle. Several deaths have been attributed to rock avalanches here, particularly in late season. It also may be necessary to pass a bergschrund above Thumb Rock saddle. Some parties make the round trip in a long day from the lodge, although bivouacking at Lake Helen improves your chances for success. Early-season ascents are recommended, as they are more enjoyable and do less damage.

West Buttress – Casaval Ridge ★ 8-10 hrs

This is the obvious ridge separating Cascade and Avalanche Gulches. It is said to be an enjoyable climb with moderate mixed climbing, and is recommended as a good winter route, safe from avalanches and rockfall.

From the lodge, head to the west side of the ridge and ascend it. A few obstacles on the ridge are fairly easily passed. This route has some third-class scrambling, and at a few spots, a rope might be desirable. Alternatively, you can reach the ridge from either of two "windows" in Avalanche Gulch. Without snow cover, this route is not recommended. Grade III, Class 4. Most parties wisely descend Avalanche Gulch, except during periods of snow instability.

Other South Side Summit Routes

Cascade Gulch (①; 8-10 hrs) is the westernmost south-side route. From the lodge, ascend west around the toe of Casaval Ridge and ascend directly up the gulch to "Shastina Saddle." From the saddle, continue east up the ridge to the summit crest. The route is difficult when icy, and fairly tedious when snow free. Rockfall and avalanche hazard.

The fine **Sargents Ridge** route (②; 8-10 hrs) ascends the obvious ridge above Ski Bowl parking area. From Ski Bowl, the route is straightforward to "Shastarama Point" (11,135 feet). Continue up the upper ridge to Thumb Rock saddle (staying on the left side of Thumb Rock). The route joins Avalanche Gulch route here. There is moderate rock scrambling, with some Class 3 or 4 sections on the upper portion of the ridge. Avalanche hazard. Grade III.

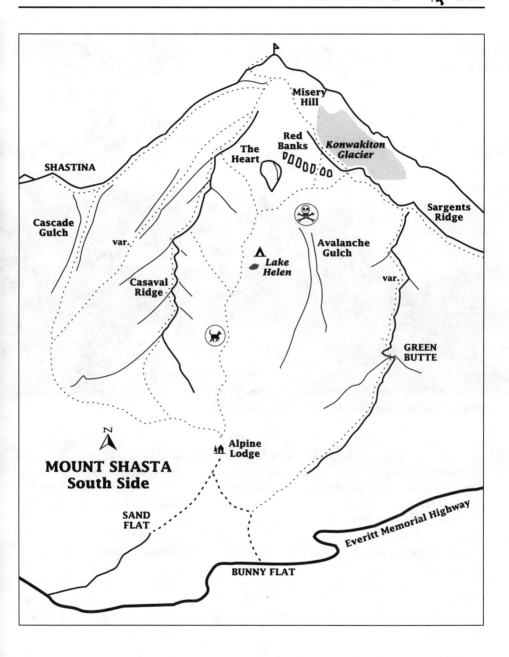

Mount Shasta's Sargents Ridge and Konwakiton Glacier.

Photo: Austin Post, U. S. Geological Survey

Clear Creek Approach

Approaches for Mud Creek, Clear Creek and Wintun Ridge routes are via Clear Creek Trail. Take State Highway 89 east from McCloud about 3 mi to Pilgrim Creek Road 13, which is followed about 5 mi to Widow Springs Road 41N15. Turn left and follow this road past Widow Springs and through an intersection with Forest Service Road 31. At a point about 1 mi farther west on Road 41N61, take the left fork and follow the spur to its end (or as far as you dare if you don't have four-wheel drive). Alternatively, drive McKenzie Butte Road 88 (which heads east from Highway 89 a few miles west of McCloud) to Road 31 (about 3 mi). Go east on Road 31 several miles, across Mud Creek Dam, to the junction with Widow Springs Road. Continue as described above. From the road end, hike Clear Creek Trail to its end. Social trails or open cross-country hiking leads to the routes.

Clear Creek Route   6-8 hrs

This route ascends the Clear Creek drainage directly to the summit shoulder. There is little difficulty or danger here, except during avalanche conditions; routefinding is very straightforward. Early-season ascents and ski descents are popular.

Mount Shasta 169

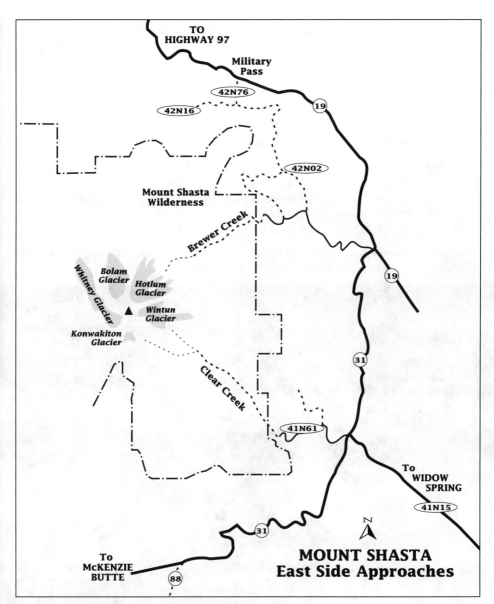

Other East Side Summit Routes

The **Konwakiton Glacier – Mud Creek** route (③; 8-10 hrs) climbs the eastern lobe of the Konwakiton Glacier. From the source springs of Clear Creek, ascend the gentle ridge between the Mud and Clear Creek drainages. The route stays left, crosses over an obvious ridge at about 11,000 feet into the Konwakiton Glacier basin, and ascends the right lobe of the glacier to Misery Hill. Rockfall and avalanche danger. Grade III, Class 3.

The **Wintun Ridge** route (◉; 8-10 hrs) ascends the ridge southeast of the Wintun Glacier. Routefinding is not difficult.

Brewer Creek Approach

Brewer Creek Trail is commonly used to get to Wintun and Hotlum Glacier routes. There are several possible routes to the trailhead, and any attempt to give directions would be confusing. The customary route usually is well-marked, so just follow the signs or refer to the map in this guide. However you go, you want to end up on Road 42N10, which leads to the trailhead.

Hotlum Glacier   10-12 hrs

This route may be approached either from Gravel Creek or Brewer Creek (better) as for the Wintun-Hotlum Route. Ascend the glacier fairly directly to 13,000 feet, then finish via one of several possible variations. One variation ascends a snow finger to Hotlum-Wintun Ridge; another skirts around the headwall on the right (mixed rock and ice); and another climbs the headwall directly (much more difficult, 5.8 rock and/or ice). Grade III.

The route has moderate avalanche danger and some rockfall exposure beneath the headwall. Crevasses can be troublesome in late season.

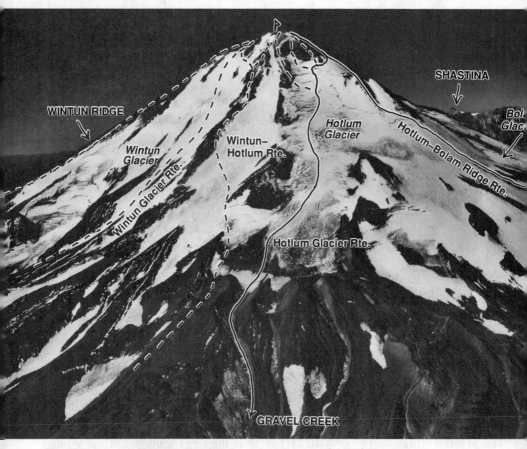

The Wintun and Hotlum Glacier dominate the east face of Shasta.

Photo: Austin Post, U.S. Geological Survey

Two other routes can be reached via Brewer Creek. The **Wintun Glacier** route (③; 8-10 hrs) is best approached by following Brewer Creek Trail to its "end" (which is well above the glacier toe at about 9,000 feet), then dropping south into Wintun Canyon. The route ascends the glacier to the south shoulder. Once past the crevasses, the route to the summit shoulder is relatively straightforward. Rockfall and avalanche hazard.

The **Wintun-Hotlum** route (②; 8-10 hrs) ascends the gentle ridge separating the Wintun and Hotlum Glaciers. Much of the route is protected from avalanches. Approach via cross-country hiking alongside Brewer Creek. Follow snowfields left of the Hotlum Glacier, then either traverse left across the upper Wintun Glacier to the south shoulder finish or ascend the "Hotlum-Wintun Ridge" to the crest just northeast of the summit.

North Gate Trail Approach

North Gate Trail reaches the Hotlum and Bolam Glacier routes. The roads approaching this trail are complex and confusing. Head north from Weed on State Highway 97 to Military Pass Road, which is followed about 7 mi to Military Pass. You will reach a prominent fork (see map for detail, since directions would be confusing here). If you stay left, you'll reach Inconstance Creek Trailhead, an alternate approach to Hotlum Glacier; the right fork, Road 42N16, goes to North Gate Trailhead, and more direct access to the Hotlam-Bolam area.

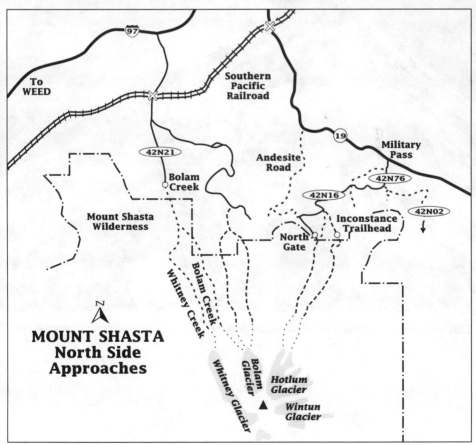

Hotlum-Bolam Ridge ★ ① 6-8 hrs

This route goes between the Hotlum and Bolam Glaciers via a gentle ridge. Approach via the North Gate trail. Ascend the ridge to a prominent step at about 13,000 feet, where the route traverses right to the Bolam Glacier route. Although this route is regarded as the safest and most reliable north-side route, there have been fatalities here. The route is often used as a descent for other north-side routes.

Bolam Glacier ★ ② 6-8 hrs

Bolam is a broad glacier on the mountain's north flank. There are several possible routes. Approach via either North Gate (longer, but recommended by some as the best), or Bolam or Whitney Creeks. Climb either the east or west upper lobes of the glacier to the summit crest. The east version joins the north ridge near 13,000 feet; the latter does not join the ridge until very near the summit. Crevasses can be a problem in late season.

This view shows the Hotlam and Bolam glaciers. Photo: Austin Post, U. S. Geological Survey

Mount Shasta 173

Whitney Creek Approach

Whitney Creek Road is the common approach to Whitney Glacier, and may be used to reach Bolam Glacier as well. Bolam Creek Road gets you closer, but is four-wheel drive only and not recommended. Whitney Creek Road 43N21 begins about 12 mi north of Weed on State Highway 97, and is followed all the way to Graham Greek Trailhead. The trail forks after 1 mi or so; go right to Whitney Creek, left to Bolam Creek. Social trails and cross-country hiking lead to the glaciers.

Whitney Glacier   10-12 hrs

Whitney is the longest glacier in California and the most impressive on Mount Shasta. Approach via either North Gate (longer, but recommended), or Whitney or Bolam Creeks.

The traditional route gains the eastern portion of the glacier's toe and ascends as crevasses dictate to the head of the glacier and the summit crest. You can ascend the prominent icefall directly, but this is not recommended during warm weather. Grade II. A variation ascends left of the glacier on snow or pumice slopes (the "Bolam-Whitney divide"), never touching glacier ice. This route is okay during early season, but in late season can seem an eternal scree slog.

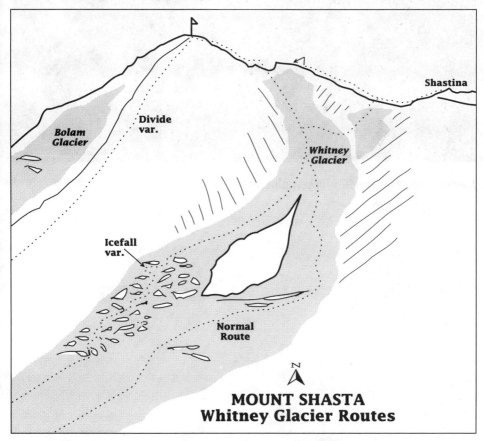

MOUNT SHASTA Whitney Glacier Routes

Lassen Peak

Lassen Peak, "the world's largest plug dome."

Photo: Alan Kearney

Chapter Eighteen:
Lassen Peak
10,457 ft./3188m

Lassen Peak, this southernmost of the Cascade volcanoes, is a minor mountain compared with the glaciated giants farther north. Its only worthwhile route is a trail leading to its summit.

Mount Lassen is the significant plug-dome remnant of a former 11,000-foot stratovolcano known as Mount Tehama (or Brokeoff Volcano). Mount Tehama collapsed and was nearly erased by ice-age glaciers, but Lassen Peak, a dacite dome, extruded itself from Tehama's remains some 11,000 years ago. In May 1914, Lassen awoke, and a year later began spilling lava, snow and mud across its slopes. On May 22, 1915, the mountain erupted violently, shooting hot gasses and ash into the stratosphere. A simultaneous lateral blast and nuée ardente (hot pyroclastic flow) devastated the northwestern part of the present-day park. This eruption, and the presence of fumaroles and 200° F mud pots nearby, signal the mountain is far from dormant.

Mount Lassen, the "largest plug dome in the world," is the centerpiece of one of California's less-crowded national parks, and is located in northeastern California about 180 miles north of Sacramento. The park may be reached via State Highway 44 east from Redding (45 miles), or via State Highway 36 east from Red Bluff, (also about 45 miles), or from the west (Susanville) via either Highway 36 or 44, (about 70 miles). State Highway 89 runs south from Mount Shasta directly through the park.

Lassen Peak is not the only volcanic peak located within Lassen Volcanic National Park. Cinder Cone (6,907 ft./2105m) is just northeast of Lassen, as is Prospect Peak (8,338 ft./2541m), a shield volcano. These and other volcanic peaks within the park also may be ascended without technical difficulty.

Surprisingly, the park does have some technical rock climbing routes. Although there are many areas of poor-quality, highly-fractured volcanic rock on and near Lassen, there also are some steep faces on solid tuff featuring routes beginning at about 5.6, and many 5.10 and harder routes. Although the park service has discouraged rock climbing since a 1977 double fatality, there is no official limitation on rock climbing at time of publication.

There is a $5-per-car charge upon entering the park. There are numerous campgrounds within the park, which cost between $5 and $7 per night. Backcountry camping requires a permit, which may be obtained upon entry to the park.

176 Lassen Peak

Further information can be obtained from:

> Lassen Volcanic National Park (916) 595-4444
> Box 100
> Mineral, California 96063

Report emergencies to Lassen Volcanic National Park, (916) 595-4444, or dial 911.

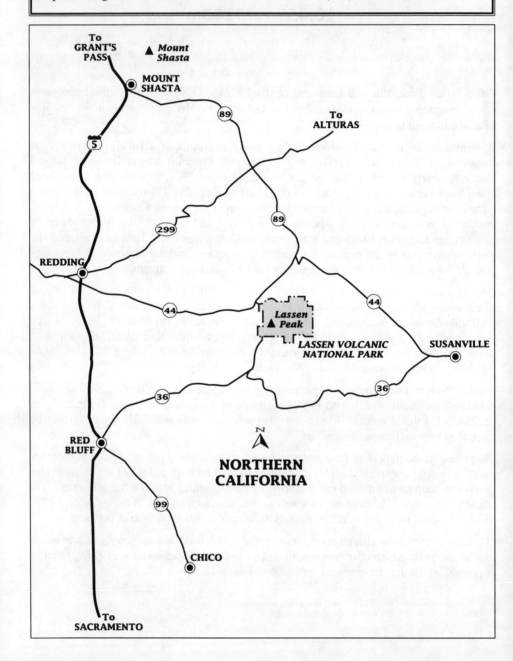

Lassen Peak   177

The Lassen Peak Trail is the customary route to the summit. The Park Service insists hikers stay on established trails. Because of this, and because the mountain itself is not technically challenging, no other routes are included in this guide. Climbers wishing to climb off-trail routes should obtain prior permission from park officials. Those wishing to explore the rock climbing within Lassen Park should consult John Bald's *Climbs of Lassen National Park and Surrounding Areas*.

Lassen Peak Trail   3-5 hrs

The well-marked Lassen Peak Trail begins about 8 mi inside the park from the southern entrance, just beyond Lake Helen. Hike the steep 2.25 miles to the summit. This is a heavily-traveled tourist trail, and park rangers lead guided hikes to the summit. There are usually no special dangers or difficulties, assuming you stay on the trail and have no health problems. Obtain a map and brochure upon entry to the park for directions.

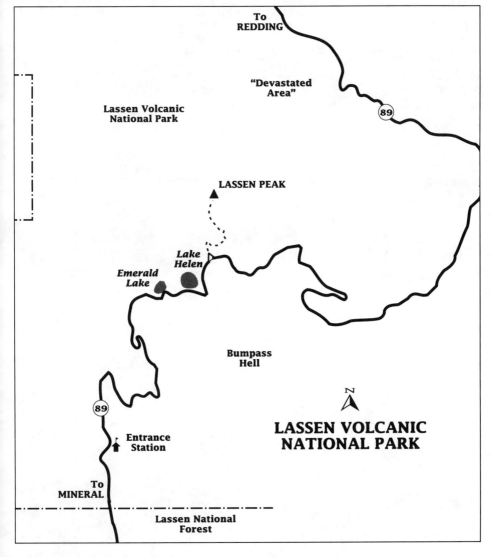

Appendix

Guide Services:

Alpine Ascents Unlimited (206) 633-0640
4013 Stone Way North
Seattle, WA 98103

American Alpine Institute (206) 671-1570
1513-A 12th Street
Bellingham, WA 98227

Mountain Ski Ventures (206) 647-0656
P.O. Box 2974
Bellingham, WA 98227

Pacific High Mountain Guides (604) 892-5859
P.O. Box 1429 (604) 892-9662
Squamish, B.C. V0N 3G0

Rainier Mountaineering, Inc. (206) 569-2775
Paradise, WA 98398

Rainier Mountaineering, Inc. (206) 627-6242
535 Dock Street, #209 (Off-Season)
Tacoma, WA 98402

Shasta Mountain Guides (916) 926-3117
1938 Hill Road
Mount Shasta, CA 96067

Timberline Mountain Guides (503) 548-0749
P.O. Box 464
Terrebonne, OR 97760

Mountaineering Clubs:

The British Columbia Mountaineering Club
P.O. Box 2674
Vancouver, B.C.
Canada V6B 3W8

The Cascadians
P.O. Box 2201
Yakima, WA 98907

The Mazamas
909 N.W. 19th Avenue
Portland, OR 97209

The Mountaineers
300 Third Avenue West
Seattle, WA 98109

The Obsidians
P.O. Box 322
Eugene, OR 97440

Washington Alpine Club
P.O. Box 352
Seattle, WA 98111

Sierra Club, Cascade Chapter
1516 Milrose Avenue
Seattle, WA 98122

Bibliography

Key: (Date) 57: (page) 1–28, also 12/89:26-37

Printed References and Books Of Interest:

American Alpine Club: *Climber's Guide to the Cascade and Olympic Mountains of Washington,* American Alpine Club, 1961

American Alpine Journal: 36:475, 39:310, 46:44, 49:143, 219 50:121, 54:23, 57:1-28, 58:78-81, 59:301, 305, 60:114-16, 121 61:336; 61:360, 62:204, 63:469-71, 64:169-70, 65:407, 66:126-28, 366-67, 67:384-86, 69:305, 338-39, 71:228, 340, 349, 72:113-14, 74:141-42, 76:441, 79:182-84.

Avalanche Echoes (B.C.): 64:4, 68:4-5, 69:4-5, 10/73:3, 12/74:7, 11/79:3, 6/80:4, 4/83:6, 2/84:2, 10/84:2.

B.C. Mountaineering Club Newsletter: 7/25:6, 6/44, 11/55, 4/66, 8/71, 9/80, 11/82:15, 6/84:30-43, 11/85:12, 12/87:5-6, 8/88:1, 42.

Bald, John: *Climbs of Lassen National Park and Surrounding Areas,* Redding, California 1990 ($10, P.O. Box 494873, Redding, CA).

Baldwin: *Exploring the Coast Mountains on Skis,* 1983.

Bauer, Jack: "The North Face of Mount Rainier," The Mountaineer No. 27, 1938.

Beckey, Fred: *Cascade Alpine Guide, Climbing and High Routes, Columbia River to Stevens Pass,* 2ed., Seattle: The Mountaineers 1987; Cascade Alpine Guide, Climbing and High Routes, Stevens Pass to Rainy Pass, Seattle: The Mountaineers 1981; Cascade Alpine Guide, Climbing and High Routes, Rainy Pass to Fraser River, Seattle: The Mountaineers 1987; Mountains of North America, San Francisco: Sierra Club Books 1982; Challenge of the North Cascades, Seattle: The Mountaineers 1977.

Bien: *Mountain Skiing,* Seattle: The Mountaineers 9/82

Biewener, Jack: "A Climber's Guide to Mt. Hood," Portland: Mazama 56:28; "A Climber's Guide to Three Sisters, Mt. Washington, and Three Fingered Jack," Mazama 55:16.

Brugman/Post: "Effects of Volcanism on the Glaciers of Mount St. Helens," U.S.G.S. Bulletin 1981.

Canadian Alpine Journal: 08:205-10, 11:175-6, 12:140, 32:90-91, 37:107-11, 57:73-4, 71:68-9, 72:71-2, 81:64-65, 86:53.

Climbing (Magazine): 5/82:13 (Little Tahoma Peak), 12/87:52-56 ("Willis Wall" by Gary Speer), 4/91:81 ("North Ridge of Mount Baker" by Alan Kearney).

Coleman: *The first ascent of Mount Baker,* Bellingham, Washington: Shorey 1966.

Crandell: "Recent Eruptive History of Mount Hood, Oregon, and Potential Hazards from Future Eruptions," USGS Bulletin 1980.

Crandell/ Mullineaux: "Volcanic Hazards at Mount Rainier, Washington," USGS Bulletin 1238.

Culbert, Dick: *Alpine Guide to Southwestern British Columbia,* 1974.

Dodge, Nick: *A Climbing Guide to Oregon,* Beaverton, Oregon: The Touchstone Press 1975; *A Climber's Guide to Oregon,* Portland: The Mazamas 1968.

Fairley, Bruce: *Climbing & Hiking in Southwestern British Columbia,* Vancouver: Gordon Soules Book Publishers 1986.

Foxworthy/Hill: *Volcanic Eruptions of 1980 at Mount St. Helens: The First 100 Days,* Geological Survey Professional Paper 1249, 1984.

Gillette/Dostal: *Cross-Country Skiing,* 3ed., Seattle: The Mountaineers 1988.

Grauer, Jack: *Mount Hood: A complete history,* 1975.

Haines: *Mountain Fever, Historic Conquests of Rainier,* Salem: Oregon Historical Society 1962.

Hall: "In Oregon It's Mount Jefferson," Off Belay No. 11, 10/73.

Harris, Stephen: *Fire Mountains of the West: The Cascade and Mono Lake Volcanoes,* Missoula: Mountain Press Publishing Company 1988.

Hazard, Joseph: *The Glacier Playfields of Mount Rainier National Park,* Seattle: Western Printing 1920

Hazard, Joseph: *Snow Sentinels of the Pacific Northwest,* Seattle: Lowman & Hanford Co., 1932.

Hildreth/Fierstein: "Mount Adams: Eruptive History of an Andeşide-Dacite Stratovolcano at the Focus of a Fundamentally Basaltic Volcanic Field," U.S.G.S. Open-File Report 85-521 1985.

Hill: "Volcano History and Geology," Off Belay No. 8, 4/73.

LaChapelle: *The ABC of Avalanche Safety,* Seattle: The Mountaineers 1986.

Bibliography

Lowe, Don & Roberta: *62 Hiking Trails — Northern Oregon Cascades,* Beaverton, Oregon: The Touchstone Press 1979; *60 Hiking Trails — Central Oregon Cascades,* Beaverton, Oregon: The Touchstone Press 1978.
Macaree: *103 Hikes in Southwest British Columbia,* Seattle: The Mountaineers, and Vancouver: Gordon Soules Book Publishers 1987.
Majors: *Mount Baker: A Chronicle of its Historic Eruptions and First Ascent,* Bellingham: Northwest Press 1978.
Manning/Spring: *50 Hikes in Mount Rainier National Park,* Seattle: The Mountaineers 1975.
Martinson: *Wilderness Above the Sound: The story of Mount Rainier National Park,* Seattle: Northland Press 1986.
Mathews: *Garibaldi Geology, A popular guide to the geology of the Garibaldi Lake area,* Vancouver: Geological Association of Canada 1975.
Mathews, Daniel: *Cascade - Olympic Natural History, a trailside reference,* Portland: Raven Editions 1988.
Matthes: *Mount Rainier and its Glaciers,* 1928.
Mazama (Club Journal): 00:1-40, 00:203-7, 03:143-47, 164-75, 05:201-34, 07:5-26, 67-69, 12:6-20, 13:1-20, 36-38, 14:1-27, 37-38, 54-62, 69-77, 15:1-24, 16:1-28, 17:127-145, 180-86, 19:301-18, 339-42, 20:3-16, 26-54, 21:9-11, 19-27, 46-7, 22:21-35, 23:21-24, 69-75, 24:32-9, 25:25-66, 32:7-23, 33:7-29, 34:29-32, 35:36-37, 36:36, 41-43, 38:13-17, 39:9-11, 53:31-36, 54:5-11, 31-36, 55:16-25, 56:28-34, 57:32-34, 58:79, 60:42-44, 52-53, 64:12-22, 65:43, 66:51-52, 67:28-30, 67-70, 68:54-56, 69:16-20, 41, 47-49, 70:28, 71:13-15, 21-23, 72:26-30, 74-77, 73:17-19, 83:30-1.
McCoy: *The Mount Adams Country — Forgotten Corner of the Columbia River Gorge,* White Salmon, Washington: Pahto Publications 1987.
McNeil: *McNeil's Mount Hood,* Zig Zag, Oregon; Zig Zag Papers, 1990.
Meany: *Mount Rainier: A Record of Exploration,* Portland: Binfords & Mort 1916.
Miles: *Koma Kulshan: The Story of Mt. Baker,* Seattle: The Mountaineers 1984; "Mount Baker - 1868," Off Belay No. 28, 8/76.
Miller: "Potential Hazards from Future Eruptions of Mount Shasta Volcano, Northern California," USGS Bulletin 1980.
Mitchell: "Arctic Mountaineering on the 47th Parallel," Off Belay No. 2, April 1972.
Molenaar, Dee: *The Challenge of Rainier,* Seattle: The Mountaineers 1987.
Mountaineer (Club Journal): 12:37, 18:49, 20:46-47, 24:57, 30:22-24, 31:12, 56-8, 33:14, 34:5, 35:3-7, 37:23, 48:50, 53, 49:1-4, 55, 54:67-68, 56:38-54, 122, 58:96-99, 101-2, 59:105, 60:76, 61:97, 99-100, 62:91-2, 98-9, 63:87-9, 64:131, 66:203-4, 68:205, 69:112, 70:108-9, 71:72-74, 75:102, 77:72, 106, 78:104.
Mountaineers, The: *Mountaineering: Freedom of the Hills,* 5ed., Seattle: The Mountaineers 1992.
Nadeau: *Highway to Paradise,* Tacoma: Valley Press 1983.
Naragon, Janice and Mason, Christopher: *Best Foot Forward,* Woodinville, Washington: GrizzlyWare (c) 1990; Washington and Oregon data bases, 10/91, 12/91.
National Geographic (Magazine): 5/63 *(Mount Rainier: Training Ground for Everest).*
National Park Service: *Mount Rainier National Park Wilderness Management Plan; Backcountry Trip Planner;* Mount Rainier National Park press releases, photo and historical archives, miscellaneous records and publications.
Off Belay (Magazine): #1:22-26, #2:30-36), #13:4-9, 51, #18:2-9, #24:10-15, #29:2-5), #34:9-23, #35:21-25, #36:5-12, #42:2-9). #1:10-13, 42, #2:7-11, 48-49, #8:41, #9:37, #12:30-35, #16:33, #17:2-10, 20-25, #20:33-35, #26:31-35, #27:51-55, #39:33, #40:31-32, #44:20-27, 30-31, #49:32, #55:22. Citations of particular interest: "Mount Adams — A History," "Mountaineering on Mount Adams," 6/72; "Mount Washington, Oregon's Outlaw," 10/72; "In Oregon, It's Mount Jefferson," 10/72, "Boom!," 6/80.
Prater: *Snowshoeing,* 3ed., Seattle: The Mountaineers 1988.
Reid: "Three-Fingered Jack — A directory and some comments," Mazama 1929.
Ream: *Northwest Volcanoes, A Roadside Geologic Guide,* Renton: B.J. Books 1983.
Roper, Steve: "Climbers' Guide to Mount Shasta," Ascent No. 2, 1968.
Rusk, C.E.: *Tales of a Western Mountaineer,* Boston and New York: Houghton Mifflin Company 1924 (reprinted 1978 by The Mountaineers with new photos, biography of C.E. Rusk, by Darryl Lloyd).
Seattle Post-Intelligencer: 1/17/91:F1-2.
Seattle Times: 6/10/91:A1-2.
Selters, Andy: *Glacier Travel and Crevasse Rescue,* Seattle: The Mountaineers 1990.
Selters/Zanger: *The Mt. Shasta Book,* Berkeley: The Wilderness Press 1989.
Shane: *Discovering Mount St. Helens,* Seattle: University of Washington Press 1985.
Snow: *Mount Rainier: The story behind the scenery,* Las Vegas: K.C. Publications Inc. 1988.
Spring/Manning: *100 Hikes in the Glacier Peak Region,* Seattle: The Mountaineers 1988; *100 Hikes in the North Cascades,* Seattle: The Mountaineers 1988; *100 Hikes in the South Cascades and Olympics,* Seattle: The Mountaineers 1985.
Roper/Steck: *Fifty Classic Climbs of North America,* San Francisco: Sierra Club Books 1979.
Summit (Magazine): 1/57:10-11, 5/62:6, 1/63:30-35, 6/64:9-11, 4/65:18-25, 5/66:15-18, 7/66:8-11, 3/67:4-7, 9/69:10-13, 9/71:16-17, 5/72:6-8, 5/73:2-7, 12/82:23, 3/85:8-10, 7/85:8-13, 9/85:28-31, 1/86:10-13, 3/86:12-21, 7/86:10-15, 7/86:4-6, 3/87:30, 11/87:21-25, 5/88:1-21.
Thomas, Jeff: *Oregon High,* Portland: Keep Climbing Press, 1991.

Bibliography 181

Tolbert: *History of Mount Rainier National Park*, Seattle: Lowman & Hanford 1933.
U.S. Forest Service: "Guide to the Mt. Baker District," Mt. Baker-Snoqualmie National Forest; U.S. Forest Service: "Climbing Mount Hood, A guide to south side routes"; Wilderness Management Plans for Mount Shasta, Three Sisters, Mount Jefferson and Mount Washington wilderness areas; TRIS.
Varsity Outdoor Club Journal: 60:11, 27, 61:10, 65:23, 65:9, 68:59, 69:17, 56, 106, 71:60, 72:13-14, 73:60, 74:16-18, 39-41, 50-2, 65-6, 75:25, 42, 44-6, 76:27-8, 78:39-40, 79:26-7, 83:71-2, 87:11-13, 88.
Washington Geologic Newsletter, Volume 15 Number 4, October 1987.
Wilkerson: *Medicine for Mountaineering*, Seattle: The Mountaineers 1986.
Wilkerson/Bangs/Hayward: *Hypothermia, Frostbite and other Cold Injuries*, Seattle: The Mountaineers 1986.
Williams, Chuck: *Mount St. Helens National Volcanic Monument*, Seattle: The Mountaineers 1988.

Personal References:

Arksey, Matt: Interviews 6/90, 7/91.
Bald, John: Telephone interviews 6/90.
Bauman, Tom: Correspondence, manuscript review 12/90.
Boyer, Tim: Interviews and correspondence, manuscript review 3/90.
Dale, Mark: Telephone interview and correspondence, manuscript review 5/90.
Dodge, Nick: Correspondence 4/91.
Doty, Steve: Telephone interview 5/91.
Emetaz, Roland: Correspondence, manuscript review 4/91.
Erschler, Phil: Correspondence, manuscript review 2/90.
Fairley, Bruce: Telephone interview and correspondence, manuscript review 3/90.
Kerchum, Wally: correspondence, manuscript review 12/90, 5/91, 8/91.
Hall, Ed: Telephone interviews and correspondence, manuscript review 11/89, 9/90.
Hentges, Cy: Telephone interviews and correspondence 4/91, 6/91.
Lloyd, Darryl: Telephone interviews and correspondence, manuscript review 3/90.
Molenaar, Dee: Telephone interview and correspondence, manuscript review 3/90.
Naragon, Janice: Interview and review of Best Foot Forward™ computer-based trail directory for Washington and Oregon, 10/91, 12/91.
Nielsen, Larry: Correspondence, manuscript review 2/90.
Olsen, Jon: Interviews and correspondence, photo review 5/91.
Olson, Garry: Correspondence, manuscript review 9/90.
Ostrowski, Dan: Interviews and correspondence 4/91, 8/91.
Samora, Barbara: Interviews and correspondence, manuscript review 4/91, 5/91.
Serl, Don: Telephone interviews and correspondence, manuscript review 10/90, 7/91.
Sorseth, Steve: Interview and correspondence, manuscript review 7/91.
Soule, Bill: Interviews and correspondence, manuscript review, 3/90, 5/91, 10/91.
Voeltz, Leif: Interview and correspondence, manuscript review 9/89, 3/90.
Weaver, Doug: Interviews and correspondence, manuscript review 9/90, 8/91.
Weaver, Howard: Interviews and correspondence, manuscript review, photo review 3/91, 4/91.
Wickwire, James: Interview and correspondence, manuscript review 2/90.
Yates, Margaret: Interviews and correspondence, manuscript review 12/90, 3/91, 4/91.
Zanger, Michael: Correspondence, manuscript review 10/89, 3/90, 2/91.

Maps Used as Reference and USGS Photograph Key (by peak):

Maps and trail information were compiled or verified with the assistance of Best Foot Forward™ computer trail software, with permission of the publisher, GrizzlyWare, 16837 N.E. 176th Street, Woodinville, WA 98072, 1-800-258-HIKE.

Mount Garibaldi:
Whistler-Garibaldi Region, Outdoor Recreation Council of B.C. #3.
Garibaldi Park, British Columbia #PSG 3.

Mount Baker:
USGS 7.5-Minute Series: Mount Baker, Baker Pass, Shuksan Arm.
Mt. Baker-Snoqualmie National Forest, USFS.
USGS Photos: R1-62-33; FR6025-139; F648-134.

Bibliography

Glacier Peak:
USGS 15 Minute Series: Glacier Peak.
USGS 7.5-Minute Series: Glacier Peak East, Glacier Peak West, Lime Mountain, Gamma Peak.
USGS Photos: FR6025-28; R1-62-93; R1-62-89.

Mount Rainier:
Mt. Rainier National Park visitors map (NPS).
Mt. Rainier National Park, USGS 1:50,000-scale topo map.
USGS 15-Minute Series: Bumping Lake.
USGS 7.5-Minute Series: Golden Lakes, Mount Wow, Mowich Lake, Mount Rainier West, Mount Rainier East, Sunrise, White River Park, Chinook Pass.
Green Trails 15-Minute Series: No. 269 ("Mt. Rainier West, Wash."), No. 270 ("Mt. Rainier East, Wash."), No. 270S ("Paradise, Wash."), P.O. Box 1271, Bellevue, WA 98009.
"Mount Rainier National Park, Washington," oblique-view pictorial landform map (Molenaar's 1986 revision).
"Hiking Map & Guide, Mount Rainier National Park," Eureka, California: Earthwalk Press 9/90 (1:50,000-scale topographic map).
Trails Illustrated: Topo No. 217 ("Mount Rainier National Park"), Evergreen, Colorado. (Topographic 1:50,000 scale, provides additional information not contained on USGS maps; and is a good, weather-resistant substitute).
USGS Photos: Little Tahoma Peak, 69R1-70.

Mount Adams:
Mt. Adams Wilderness, USFS.
USGS 7.5-Minute Series: Mount Adams West, Mount Adams East.
USGS Photos: R2-62-52; R2-62-59; 67R7-82; R2-62-66; 581303.

Mount Saint Helens:
Mt. St. Helens National Volcanic Monument, USFS.
USGS 7.5-Minute Series: Mount St. Helens.
USGS Photos: 80S3-172; 80S3-109; 82S1-146.

Mount Hood:
Mt. Hood Wilderness, USFS.
USGS 7.5-Minute Series: Mt. Hood North, Mt. Hood South.
USGS Photos: 80H1-113; 80H1-109; R21-16.

Mount Jefferson:
Mt. Jefferson Wilderness, USFS.
USGS 7.5-Minute Series: Mt. Jefferson.
USGS Photos: R21-45; R21-39; R21-47; R21-43.

Three Fingered Jack:
USGS 7.5-Minute Series: Three Fingered Jack.

Mount Washington:
USGS 7.5-Minute Series: Mt. Washington.
Mt. Washington Wilderness, USFS.

Three Sisters/Broken Top:
Three Sisters Wilderness, USFS.
USGS 7.5-Minute Series: Three Sisters North, Three Sisters South, Trout Creek Butte, Lake Geneva.
USGS Photos: R21-84; 72R1-026; R21-67; K649-30; R21-81; R21-75; 61K8-92; K649-36.

Mount Thielsen:
USGS 7.5-Minute Series: Diamond Lake, Mt. Thielsen.

Mount McLoughlin:
USGS 7.5-Minute Series: Mt. McLoughlin, Lake of the Woods.

Mount Shasta:
Mt. Shasta Wilderness, USFS.
USGS 7.5-Minute Series: Mt. Shasta.
Mount Shasta Climber's Review: A summary of climbing routes on Mount Shasta, Mt. Shasta: The Fifth Season 1989.
USGS Photos: 72R1-108; 72R1-113; 72R1-129.

Lassen Peak:
Lassen Volcanic National Park visitors' map.
USGS 7.5-Minute Series: Lassen Pk., Manzanita Lake.

USGS Photo (used in Introduction): 671060